KETO KIDS LUNCH: PARENTS EDITION

TACKLING CHILD OBESITY ONE DAY AT A TIME, WITH 40 EASY-TO-MAKE DELICIOUS BREAKFAST, LUNCH, AND DINNER RECIPES, PERFECT FOR SCHOOL AND AT HOME.

EVA ILIANA

CONTENTS

Introduction   5

1. What is All the Hype About the Keto Diet?   15
2. How Do I Get my Child to Start Eating Healthy?   31
3. Pros and Cons of the Diet for Kids   44
4. Proper Meal Prep for Kids on Keto   63
5. Ketogenic Breakfast Recipes for Kids   91
6. Ketogenic Lunch Recipes   150
7. Ketogenic Dinner Recipes   191

Conclusion   243
References   249

© Copyright 2020 - All rights reserved.

The content contained within this book may not be reproduced, duplicated or transmitted without direct written permission from the author or the publisher.

Under no circumstances will any blame or legal responsibility be held against the publisher, or author, for any damages, reparation, or monetary loss due to the information contained within this book, either directly or indirectly.

Legal Notice:

This book is copyright protected. It is only for personal use. You cannot amend, distribute, sell, use, quote or paraphrase any part, or the content within this book, without the consent of the author or publisher.

Disclaimer Notice:

Please note the information contained within this document is for educational and entertainment purposes only. All effort has been executed to present accurate, up to date, reliable, complete information. No warranties of any kind are declared or implied. Readers acknowledge that the author is not engaged in the rendering of legal, financial, medical or professional advice. The content within this book has been derived from various sources. Please consult a licensed professional before attempting any techniques outlined in this book.

By reading this document, the reader agrees that under no circumstances is the author responsible for any losses, direct or indirect, that are incurred as a result of the use of the information contained within this document, including, but not limited to, errors, omissions, or inaccuracies.

INTRODUCTION

Modern life is all about convenience and comfort. From ready to eat food to pre-packaged meals, everything is readily available these days. However, this comfort and convenience certainly comes with a hefty price tag. The price we all pay for this comfort is our health.

The global human population suffers from a variety of chronic health conditions, which are all diet-related. From poor heart health to digestion troubles, and even obesity, there is a steady decline in human health. All this is primarily caused due to our poor diet.

The simplest way to fix this problem is to make sure that you consume a healthy diet right from your

INTRODUCTION

childhood. But, if you haven't been eating healthy since you were young, now is a good time to switch to healthy eating habits and make sure you introduce the same habits in your children.

When you instill healthy eating habits at a young age, they will be imbibed in your child for life. A healthy child will turn into a healthy adult. It's not just important that your child consumes healthy meals at home, but they need to make healthy eating choices when they are out of the home, too. Most school lunches are filled with unhealthy fried foods, sugars, and carbs that your child's body doesn't require and these foods eventually lead to obesity and other health risks.

As a parent, it is your responsibility to ensure your child's overall well-being. A major part of this is the food your child consumes. If their diet predominantly consists of junk or processed food, it will not do their body much good. Junk food is not just rich in calories, but it doesn't contain any nutritional value. So, your child merely piles on calories without any nourishment that their growing body needs.

Nutrition plays a vital role, especially during your child's formative years. This is one of the reasons why the diet your child consumes in their childhood tends to affect their overall health in the future. A poor diet filled with convenience foods can lead to childhood obesity and a variety of health problems that will follow your child into adulthood. If you want to raise a healthy child, then pay attention to their diet.

If you want your child to eat healthily instead of depending on junk food, then this book is perfect for you. The first step to control your child's diet is to make certain changes. Instead of allowing them to consume a diet that's rich in calories, carbs, and all things undesirable, shift to the keto diet. The ketogenic diet is an incredibly simple eating protocol. It encourages the consumption of healthy fats and discourages carb intake. Unfortunately, humans demonize fats and glorify carbs. Research done in the last couple of decades denotes that healthy fats are good for your health, and it is carbs that are harmful. So, a diet which increases the consumption of healthy fats and discourages carbohydrates is good for your child as well.

A common problem that a majority of parents face is they aren't aware of how to make their child eat healthy. Also, not a lot of parents have the time to cook healthy meals at home. It is not surprising that

INTRODUCTION

plenty of parents depend on ready to eat and junk food to feed their kids. These convenience foods certainly provide an easy way out, but it is extremely unhealthy.

In this book, you will learn about the keto diet, and the different health benefits it offers children. Once you go through the list of benefits and understand the facts about this diet, it will certainly change your perception about nutrition. You will not just learn about this diet, but will also find many delicious ketogenic recipes in this book. These recipes are extremely simple and easy to cook.

You will also learn about meal prep and simple tips you can use to prep for all the meals you wish to cook. When cooking becomes easier, it automatically becomes easier to feed your child healthy meals. You don't need any fancy ingredients or to splurge on expensive ready-made meals. All you need is the will to do it, the patience to learn about the ketogenic diet protocol, and the knowledge to cook healthy meals for your child.

As a parent of two girls, I realize the importance of nutrition. Both my girls are in school and I constantly worry about different things associated with their life. It is not just their grades or their future, but as a parent, I know I need to pay attention to their nutrition requirements, too. Kids these days lead hectic lives; from school work to extracurriculars, they have plenty to do.

In order to do all this, their bodies require sufficient fuel which comes from the food they eat. So, it is incredibly important to pay attention to your child's nourishment. It's not just about eating the right meals, but your child must make healthy choices, too. It is your responsibility to teach your child about healthy eating patterns and good decision-making when it comes to food.

Several fast-food options are readily available in the school cafeteria, and there is plenty of pressure to give your child the money to purchase junk food. It can be quite tempting too, considering the comfort it offers. However, it isn't a good idea, especially if you want to improve your child's overall health.

I believe that making healthy choices has a snowball effect. It not only gives your child's body the nourishment it needs, but it will also make your child feel better about themselves, not just physically, but mentally as well. This, in turn, will show a positive change in different aspects of their life, ranging from academics to extracurricular activities. Since you

INTRODUCTION

have the power to mold your child's physical and mental well-being, it is time you make the most of this opportunity that's available.

The ketogenic or keto diet is a very simple eating protocol. The first step is to arm yourself with all the important information about the keto diet. Once you understand the different benefits it offers and how it works, it becomes easier to get your child on board. There are several benefits this diet offers, such as it can reduce your child's chances of childhood obesity, and improve their overall fitness level. Apart from these, it will improve your child's cardiovascular health, promote better digestion and absorption of nutrients, stabilize energy levels, and improve cognition.

When your child starts to feel better about themselves physically and mentally, it will make them happier. Life at home becomes easy when you have a happy child. All this is possible, and you can make it a reality if you make a couple of simple dietary changes.

It isn't the easiest thing to get a child to try new things. Some children are quite fussy about the foods they eat and can pose a problem. However, it is not impossible to get them to make healthier choices. If the food looks and tastes good, why would a child resist?

Let go of any misconceptions you might have about diet food. Diet food doesn't have to be bland or tasteless. Once you experiment with the recipes, you will understand how delicious keto really is.

In this book, you'll find plenty of delicious and nutritious recipes to cook for breakfast, lunch, and dinner. All of these recipes are good for not just the meals your child has at home, but can be packed as school lunches, too. With these recipes, you can ensure that you, your child, and everyone else in the house eats healthy and nutritious meals daily.

I know making all these changes can be a little tricky. However, with patience, persistence, and a little effort, everything is possible in life. I have dealt with my children and they were initially fussy and skeptical about the new diet. However, once they tasted the delicious keto food, they quickly changed their minds about it.

I know that the expertise and knowledge I gained from this experience will help you and your child as well. Your child won't pester you for a cheeseburger or a Subway sandwich ever again. In fact, with these

INTRODUCTION

simple recipes, you can quickly whip up food that looks and tastes like something right out of a restaurant's kitchen. Your child will be envied at school, and every other kid will want to share their lunch.

If you want to change your child's eating habits, then there is no time like the present. You can get started with this diet immediately; it isn't difficult. Even if your child resists, keep in mind that resistance is temporary. Most children don't usually like to try anything new, especially when it comes to the food they eat. Therefore, you need to be patient and persistent. Don't give up and keep trying, because the results will be worth your while. If you give up early, remember that you are encouraging the unhealthy eating patterns and poor food choices which will follow your child into adulthood.

Now, all you have to do is get started and delve into the world of the ketogenic diet. All the information you require about this diet is presented in a clear and easy to understand format in this book. Even if you are an absolute novice when it comes to cooking, you will be able to manage these recipes.

When you start using the recipes given in this book, your child will not be able to resist the delicious home cooked meals. Once they get used to this diet, you can rest easy knowing that their body will be getting all the nourishment it needs. Also, be prepared to be pleasantly surprised with the wonderful results this diet promises.

So, let's read on.

1

WHAT IS ALL THE HYPE ABOUT THE KETO DIET?

History of the Ketogenic Diet

One of the latest dietary trends to take the world of fitness and health by storm is the ketogenic diet. In fact, it has become a buzzword these days. It is a low carb and high-fat eating protocol, which has gained the attention of mainstream media and culture. In this section, you will learn about the meaning of the ketogenic diet, its history, how it works, and some popular misconceptions about the keto diet.

The keto diet protocol was initially used to treat epilepsy in children who did not respond to medications. According to Hippocrates, believed to be the father of modern medicine, fasting was the only prescribed treatment for epilepsy. In fact, it was considered to be a standard practice to treat epilepsy across the world for almost 2000 years. Ancient Greek physicians often advocated dietary restrictions for their patients to treat conditions such as epilepsy. Therefore, fasting became an integral part of a healthy lifestyle practiced in ancient Greece.

These days, most people use the keto diet as a tool for weight loss. However, the origin of this diet strategy is based on its involvement in the treatment of epilepsy. The first modern study about fasting and its role in epilepsy was conducted in France sometime during 1911. In this study, it was noticed that the patients who consumed a low-calorie diet and fasted for prolonged periods experienced fewer seizures and lead a relatively healthier life when compared with others who didn't fast or follow a low-cal diet.

Around this time, Hugh Conklin, an American osteopathic physician, started to recommend fasting as a treatment to help his epileptic patients control seizures. In fact, he recommended his patients fast for anywhere between 18 and 25 days at a stretch. He noted an incredible success rate to treat epilepsy in adults and an even better rate in children. This led to the conclusion that fasting for prolonged periods is a great way to treat epilepsy.

These results certainly seemed quite impressive. However, there was one small yet obvious issue with this treatment: what would happen if the patients stopped fasting? If the patients stopped fasting or went back to their usual diets, the seizures returned. Therefore, even though it was an effective treatment, it was not considered to be practical or even sustainable in the long run.

So, several other doctors tried to replicate these results, and some started to experiment with different types of diets. Instead of eliminating all calories, they tried out a variety of combinations to reduce the intake of calories. During one such experiment, Dr. Wilder at the Mayo Clinic noticed that the seizures in epilepsy patients who had low blood sugar levels were low. He noticed that these patients followed a low carb and a high-fat diet, and it helped reduce the seizures they experienced. He worked to create a diet that mimicked the fasting metabolism without enduring fasting for prolonged periods. And that is how the ketogenic diet was invented.

What is the Keto Diet?

The keto diet is a low carb and a high-fat diet, and it certainly is not a new concept. While on this diet, you must ensure that your child eats fewer carbs than normal, maintains moderate intake of protein, and increases their intake of healthy fats. When their carb intake reduces, it puts their body in a metabolic state known as ketosis. In this state, their body starts to burn fats from the food they consumed to fuel itself.

The term keto in the ketogenic diet comes from the small fuel molecules the body produces to keep itself going, known as ketones. Ketones are used as an alternative fuel source for glucose that the body usually uses. The ketogenic diet prescribes that 70% of daily calories should be derived from fats, about 20% from proteins, and less than 10% from carbs.

Scientists are not yet 100% certain of how the keto diet works. A popular albeit rudimentary theory is that the natural structure of ketones triggers an anti-electrical effect on the brain. Seizures are usually caused by abnormal electrical impulses and an anti-electrical effect can help prevent seizures from occurring.

Once this diet started to gain popularity as a treatment option for epilepsy, doctors started to notice several other benefits of ketosis. They believed that it not only helped control seizures, but children who were on this diet were less irritable, easier to discipline, and more alert than others. Also, it was noticed that these children managed to get good sleep at night and were more energetic.

Despite all its success, the keto diet was soon pushed into obscurity with the popularity of anticonvulsant drugs. This diet was forgotten for a while, and even when people practiced it, they didn't do it properly, which gave the diet a bad name.

During the 90s, not a lot of people were aware of the ketogenic diet. At this time, a popular television show featured on American networks, titled

Dateline. In fact, *Dateline* gets most of the credit because it reintroduced the concept of the ketogenic diet to Americans. In one episode, which aired in October 1994, the ketogenic diet was used to treat seizures in a two-year-old kid named Charlie. Charlie had epilepsy and his seizures were uncontrollable; then he was introduced to the keto diet. Charlie sought treatment at John Hopkins, and he was administered the keto diet. Soon, the world watched as his seizures slowed down and it triggered a lot of scientific interest in this eating strategy.

Once the scientific community regained interest in this diet, the rest was history. It soon became one of the most popular diets known to human society. From weight loss to better health and treatment of epilepsy, this diet has multiple benefits.

Decoding the Keto Diet

Any food that contains carbs or sugar is immediately converted into glucose upon consumption. This conversion takes place with the help of an enzyme known as insulin, which is secreted by the pancreas. Insulin helps regulate the levels of blood sugar, with the transportation of glucose produced. Once glucose is produced, it is transported to different cells in the body. However, due to evolution or biological changes, the human body doesn't immediately use all the energy it produces. Instead, only a portion of this energy is used, and the rest is stored as fat molecules. These fat molecules are first stored in the liver, and when the liver runs out of storage space, they are stored as fat deposits in different cells in the body.

Over a period, this unnecessary accumulation of excess energy leads to weight gain, and obesity in extreme cases. This is one reason why you must pay attention to your child's diet.

When your child's carb consumption reduces, the production of ketones from fats increases. These ketones become the primary source of fuel for all the cells in their body and especially the ones in their brain. The brain requires a constant supply of energy and it cannot sustain itself on direct fats, but it can survive on glucose or ketones. This is one of the reasons why your child's energy levels will finally stabilize once their body gets used to ketosis. In ketosis, their body keeps burning fats unless they consume any excess carbs.

Here is a simple example to get a better understanding of how ketosis works. Think of a boulder on top of a hill. Once the boulder is pushed, it starts rolling down the slope, and will keep rolling and gaining momentum until something stops it. This is pretty much how ketosis works and how the body produces ketones. It keeps producing ketones until your child's carb intake increases beyond the desired limit. This is one of the reasons why it is important to pay close attention to your child's carb intake. If they consume excess carbs or proteins, it will effectively kick their body out of ketosis.

On the keto diet, your child's entire body switches its fuel supply from glucose to fats. These fats are constantly burned to provide energy. Whenever their insulin levels reduce, their ability to burn fats increases. Lower levels of insulin make it easier to access all the reserves of fats present in the body. This is the primary reason why the keto diet often leads to weight loss.

If you are advised by your child's medical care providers that they need to lose weight, then you can consult with them about the ketogenic diet. Apart from weight loss, there are other benefits to this diet, and you will learn more about these benefits in the subsequent chapters.

Myths About the Ketogenic Diet

Starchy foods are an incredibly important part of our meals. However, high carb meals are never good for your child's overall well-being. Unfortunately, it is difficult for many parents to think about making their child follow a low carb eating pattern. But what is the point of encouraging your children to eat carbs when they are not good for their body? Instead, it is time to shift to a low carb and high-fat diet such as the ketogenic diet. As with adults, even kids will greatly benefit from a diet that's low in processed carbs, sugars, and everything unhealthy. In this section, let's look at some of the most common myths associated with the keto diet.

Myth #1: It Harms Their Growth

It is a common misconception that children need carbs for their growth and that their growth will be stunted without carbs. Well, if you take a moment and logically think about this claim, you will realize that all the micronutrients, vitamins, and minerals your child needs for their growing body are present in a low carb diet. They don't need to binge on starchy foods rich in carbs and sugars to grow. There are various other and in fact, better, sources of micronutrients, and all essential nutrients such as full-fat dairy products, meat, nuts, low sugar fruit and vegetables that your child can eat. Keep in mind that the ketogenic diet is a low carb diet, and not a no carb diet. Your child will still get all the three macronutrients they need and every other micronutrient on this diet. So, you don't have to worry about their growth.

Myth #2: Carbs are Important for the Brain

A popular misconception is that carbs are essential to help the brain function optimally. You might have come across different articles that claim that the brain requires glucose to function. Well, this is only partially correct. It is true that certain parts of the brain require glucose to function, but they can also function very well on ketones the body produces on a low carb diet. It is wrong to think that children need the kind of carbs they consume these days. Keep in mind that the ketogenic diet is a low carb diet and your child will get the proper nutrition they require to function optimally. So, even if their brain needs carbs, a well-balanced keto diet provides the essential carbs.

Myth #3: Carbs are Filling

A child doesn't necessarily need to eat carbs to feel full. Take a moment before you jump to any conclusions, and you will realize this is also a misconception. Do you feel full after you eat a bag of chips for lunch, or a steak? If you eat chips, chances are you will feel full for a while and will feel hungry within no time. If you eat a hearty steak, you will not be hungry until your next meal. The same logic applies to kids, too. Carbs are unhealthy. The myth that carbs are essential to fill up a child's tummy is the primary reason why this generation is severely overfed yet undernourished. So, don't bulk up your kid's meals with starchy foods, and instead give them food that will sustain them in a healthy manner. Increase the number of healthy fats and proteins your child eats and they will feel full for longer.

Myth #4: Carbs are Important to a Child's Nutritional Needs

The growing body of a child needs healthy and wholesome meals and not empty carbs. Empty carbs are rich in calories and devoid of any nutritional value. Ensure that your child eats meals that are nutrient-dense and not devoid of nutrients. Also, understand that the ketogenic diet does include all the carbs you child needs. However, the only difference is that these carbs come from nutritional sources such as nuts, vegetables, dairy, and fruit. Instead of eating bread, your child will eat a variety of healthy and wholesome foods that are good for them.

Myth #5: Children Need Carbs for Energy

It is a popular misconception that carbs are the only form of macronutrients that provide energy. Keep in mind that every type of food gives some form of energy. A diet rich in high carbs will give your child a quick burst of energy. Try to understand that this burst of energy is short-lived. Any instant spike in your child's glucose levels will be followed by a crash. This slump in sugar levels induces more cravings for sugar and carbs. On a low carb diet, you can avoid any severe fluctuations in your child's energy and blood sugar levels. Once these levels stay stable, your child will feel energetic throughout the day and will not crave sugary treats. Foods rich in natural fats take a while to get digested. Your child's body will get a constant supply of energy as it slowly digests the food they consumed.

Myth #6: Fats Will Make Children Fat

All fats are not equal. There are some fats that are healthy, while the rest are not. For instance, the fats present in unhealthy fried things are bad for your child's health. On the other hand, the fats in naturally fatty foods such as nuts and fatty fish are good. In the ketogenic diet, all that matters is the kind of fats your child consumes. If their diet is filled with healthy fats and is low in carbs, it will not make them fat. Instead, it will lead to weight loss.

Healthy fats are important for optimal functioning of the brain, development of tissue, appetite regulation, absorption of fat-soluble vitamins, and hormone production. The chances of obesity in children on a high carb and high-fat diet are extremely high. Healthy fats help your child feel full for longer. When their tummy is full for longer, their urge to binge on snacks will reduce.

Myth #7: It Eliminates a Food Group

There are three macronutrients, namely carbs, proteins, and fats. The ketogenic diet is a well-balanced diet that includes all of these macronutrients. So, rest easy because you are not eliminating any of the important macros from your child's diet. While on a keto diet, about 70 to 75% of their daily calorie needs come from fatty foods, 20% from proteins, and the rest from carbs. You merely need to reduce the percentage of carbs they eat and increase their intake of naturally fatty foods. When you don't eliminate carbs, you don't have to worry about an unbalanced diet.

Myth #8: Low Carb Means No Fruit

All fruits that are extremely sweet are usually rich in carbs. It is true for tropical fruits such as pineapples, bananas, grapes, and mangoes. However, a low carb diet doesn't mean it is devoid of fruit. Instead, most of the carbs that your child consumes on the ketogenic diet come from healthy low carb fruits. Some of the fruits that you can easily add to your child's diet include all sorts of berries. Most berries are not only rich in antioxidants, nutrients, and minerals, but are also low in calories. Your child can certainly have a small bowl full of berries daily and get their daily intake of required fruits. On the ketogenic diet, all that matters is the types of carbs they consume.

Myth #9: Low-carb Meals are Difficult to Cook

A popular misconception is that low carb meals are incredibly difficult to cook. This myth basically stems from the fact that most of the meals we usually consume are filled with unhealthy sugars and carbs. For instance, if someone is used to having pizza three times a week and pasta on other days, a low carb meal might sound difficult. However, there is no need to worry about these things as far as the keto diet is concerned.

The best part about the keto diet is the versatility it offers. You just need to get a little creative and think outside the box. These days, there's plenty of awareness about the importance of healthy meals and diets. So, there are various keto alternatives available for regular sugars and carbs. If you're willing to get a little creative and experiment with your diet, you will realize that there is plenty to choose from. If your child loves spaghetti and meatballs, serve meatballs on a bed of zucchini noodles instead of regular noodles. Or perhaps you can substitute pizza crust with a base made of almond flour.

You don't have to worry about inspiration or variety when it comes to the ketogenic diet. There are several healthy and delicious keto-friendly recipes given in this book. All you need to do is merely gather the required ingredients, and start cooking.

As a parent, you must have all the information before you make any decisions about your child's eating patterns. Now that you have gone through the different facts and myths associated with the ketogenic diet, you are in a better position to decide whether this diet is good or bad. In fact, you would have realized that most of the fears associated with low-carb diets are baseless and absurd. It is now time to make some healthy changes to your child's diet!

2

HOW DO I GET MY CHILD TO START EATING HEALTHY?

Importance of a Healthy Diet

For the health and growth of your child, nutrition and diet are essential. A child's body requires lots of nutrients to support the growth and development of important tissues and functions. From the primary functioning of the brain to behavioral patterns, everything is influenced by the diet a child consumes. Nutrition can also help prevent certain childhood diseases such as obesity, or even diabetes.

The health benefits of a good diet result in brain development, reduction of obesity rates, healthy growth, and healthier choices in life. It is believed that poor nutrition can restrict the development of a child's brain and hinder IQ levels. It can also cause behavioral problems and reduce a child's attention span. Yes, the food you eat most certainly affects the way you feel. For instance, how do you feel after you eat a greasy cheeseburger? You will probably feel tired and lethargic. Now, how would you feel if you had a bowl of salad? You feel light and energetic. Well, this holds true for your child as well. Therefore, learn to be a little mindful of all that they eat, and you will see a positive change in their overall health.

The human body requires plenty of nourishment to grow, especially during childhood. However, the nutrients it needs should be provided to help with the growth and development of muscles and bones in the body. If your child's diet is devoid of the vital nutrients, then it will not provide their body the nutrients it needs to grow. It is believed that obesity affects about one in every three children. Obesity is not just harmful by itself, but it is also a risk factor for various chronic health conditions such as diabetes, high blood pressure, and cholesterol. When your child consumes a healthy diet, it helps set a benchmark for them, which helps ensure that they make healthier choices throughout their life.

A healthy diet contains plenty of protein, dairy, fruits, and vegetables and is devoid of added sugars, unnecessary carbs, and harmful fats. Now that you're aware of all the different benefits this diet offers, let's look at simple steps you can follow to ensure that your child consumes healthy meals.

Practical Tips for Healthier Eating Habits

As a mother, I realize the importance of nutrition for children. As a parent, I also realize how difficult it can be to make your child eat healthy food all the time. Junk food is certainly tasty and delicious. Therefore, it is no wonder that so many children love it more than healthy foods they are supposed to eat. It is quite easy to talk to adults and make them change their diets. When it comes to children, it is not that simple and is anything but straightforward.

It can be a challenge, and this is why you need to get creative and patient. There might be plenty of reasons why you want to make your child follow a low carb and high-fat diet such as the keto diet. So, whenever you feel like you cannot make your child eat healthily, remind yourself of these reasons.

There might have been instances in the past when you felt guilty about your child's diet. You probably realized the importance of getting your child to eat healthy meals, but you weren't sure how to do it. It is one thing to realize the importance of healthy eating habits, but it is an entirely different ballgame to get your child to eat healthier. It can be a little challenging, and every parent has to go through trial and error to figure out a perfect method of eating that works well not just for them, but for children as well. So, don't worry if you feel a little lost. In this section, you will learn about some simple and practical tips you can use to ensure that your child eats healthy and wholesome meals.

Schedule is Important

Children need to eat after every couple of hours to keep up with the energy demands of their growing bodies. This usually means they require three meals, two snacks, and plenty of fluids. If your child gets their nourishment from healthy and well-balanced meals, they will not be hungry all the time. When they are well fed, their energy levels will stay stabilized and they will not experience any mood swings. Ensure that you always have a couple of keto-friendly snacks on hand. Whenever your child feels hungry, you can give them one of these healthy snacks instead of junk food. Try to make a schedule and implement it. Don't allow your child to snack whenever they want, or as much as they want between meals. If your child has a schedule, they will know when they're supposed to eat and not eat. It may take some time to get used to this habit initially, but in the long run, it will work in their favor.

Cook for the Family

A common mistake plenty of parents make is that they cook separate meals for their kids. Every parent is guilty of doing this at one point or another. You probably do this because you know your child doesn't like certain foods or that they're a picky eater. Regardless of the reason, don't do this. It is not just exhausting, but it doesn't encourage your child to develop a healthy relationship with food. Don't become a short-order cook for your children. Keep in mind that children usually mimic the behavior of adults around them. Instead of cooking separate meals, cook and serve one meal for the entire family. When your child sees everyone eating the same food, they will be more inclined to try new foods. Also, it is less stressful and easier to cook.

Dinners Matter

Do you feel overwhelmed whenever you need to plan the weekly menu? If yes, then why don't you break down this task into something easier? Instead of planning the meals for seven days, try to do this for two or three days. Keep in mind that a good meal doesn't necessarily have to be fancy. The one principle you must follow to create healthy and well-balanced meals for your little ones is to include all the important macronutrients, such as low carb vegetables or a small portion of regular carbs, plenty of healthy fats from meats, dairy, or poultry, and sufficient protein. If there are any recipes that you can cook ahead and store for later, then do it. If you want to feed your children healthy meals throughout the week, meal prepping and batch cooking are your allies.

Keep Calm

Try to be neutral when it comes to your child's eating habits. Don't force them to eat something, and certainly don't punish them if they don't. It can be quite tempting to tell your child to eat their vegetables, and to be an enforcer. Instead, try to be neutral, and give them a well-balanced meal to eat. If you try to play the role of a food enforcer, it is quite likely your child will resist. Instead, set certain ground rules like no one in the house is allowed to waste anything that is served on their plate. According to this rule, your child is required to eat their share of vegetables, and you don't even have to tell them to do this. If you notice that your child prefers some meals to others, make note of it. Perhaps you can include more ingredients they like in their regular meals.

Breakfast Matters

Breakfast matters a lot, especially for growing children. Don't encourage your child to skip breakfast and ensure that they eat healthy and wholesome meals in the morning. Don't give them any processed foods such as cereals or sugary treats for breakfast. Instead, offer full-fat yogurt and some berries. You can make a breakfast smoothie, keto-friendly pancakes, eggs in different styles, and so on. There are several options, and all it takes is a little planning. If you plan the meals, it becomes easier to stock up on all the required ingredients. If all the ingredients you need are available and prepped, cooking becomes a breeze.

Don't be in a Hurry

If you want to make a child eat healthier foods, it means you need to introduce certain new foods to their diet. Don't do this all at once. Instead, slowly add a couple of new ingredients to their meals. If you introduce the new foods gradually, it will reduce their resistance toward trying out such meals. Keep in mind that it isn't necessary for your child to immediately jump on board with any idea you suggest.

For instance, if you notice that your child refuses to eat peas, try a simple technique of hero worship. Why don't you tell them that their favorite super-hero, sports player, movie star, or anyone else they admire also loves peas? This will give your child the necessary encouragement to try new foods! If you are worried that your child's food isn't nutritious, always consult a pediatrician before you add any supplements.

Get Creative

There are plenty of adults who struggle to eat their share of Brussels sprouts or even kale salads. So, why should you expect anything different from children? To ensure that your child eats all vegetables they're supposed to, you need to get a little creative. There are several different techniques to cook food, and you should try them.

If your children like dips, then serve dips, such as hummus, yogurt dressings, salsa, or even ranch salad as a dip with crudités. If you merely change the way you cook certain foods, you can make them healthier and tastier. On a keto diet, your child is free to eat plenty of healthy fats. Fats are tasty and if you are a little wise about it, you can make your child eat all the healthy foods you want them to, without any trouble. Keep an open mind, learn to get creative with different ingredients, and try the various recipes given in this book.

Involvement

A simple way to get your child excited about the meals they have is to make them feel more involved in them. Allow them to participate in not just planning for the meals, but also cooking. There are certain simple tasks you can give them, such as washing the vegetables, peeling, or maybe even handing out the required ingredients to you from the pantry. Ensure that the tasks you give them are age-appropriate. When your child feels more involved in these activities, they will feel that their opinion matters. Even if it seems like a small thing to you, your little one will appreciate it. Wherever you go shopping for groceries, take them with you. It also helps them see where the food comes from.

Replace Junk Food

If you want your child to eat healthily, it means you need to eliminate junk food. However, if you eliminate all junk food that your child is used to eating without any replacement, they might not be fine with that. To avoid any unnecessary resistance and hassle, try to replace junk food. If your child loves cookies, you can bake them keto cookies using almond flour, or any other nut-based flour. Don't eliminate junk food; instead, replace it with healthy yet tasty food that will entice your child. Things like regular potato chips and wafers can be replaced with baked kale chips.

Occasional Treats

Even if you replace junk food with healthier alternatives, ensure that your child gets to enjoy a couple of occasional treats. Keep in mind that these traits need to be occasional and not regular. Allow your child to eat some chocolate once in a while, or ice cream, or anything else that they love. If you don't let them indulge in some of their cravings, they will feel deprived. They might also resent the diet because of all this. Don't let it come to that and try to maintain moderation. Moderation is quintessential in every aspect of your life, and parenting is not an exception.

Adjust Your Attitude

You are an adult and therefore, you need to behave like an adult. You cannot expect your child to immediately understand everything that you tell them, even if it is for their own good. Instead, keep an open attitude towards them and expect a couple of setbacks. Whenever you face a hurdle, remind yourself that whatever you are doing right now is for the well-being of your child. One fear you must let go of is the fear of fat. Fats are your friends, and they are not the cause of all health problems. Healthy dietary fats will improve your child's overall health. Likewise, don't demonize carbs. Try to maintain a neutral attitude toward food. Your attitude determines your child's attitude toward food to a certain degree.

Be a Role Model

Children copy the behavior of adults around them and they learn a lot from such behaviors. Therefore, be mindful of your behavior, especially when you are around your child. If you don't like certain foods and don't eat them, don't be surprised if your child does the same. As with your attitude, ensure that you show your child proper behavior.

Now that you know all the different tips, it is time to implement them one at a time. You cannot implement these steps all at once, though. Try to do it slowly. If the change is sudden, your child might not be able to get accustomed to it. Keep in mind the old saying "slow and steady wins the race" when it comes to the ketogenic diet.

3

PROS AND CONS OF THE DIET FOR KIDS

The keto diet is a simple protocol that offers a variety of health benefits. Unlike other severely restrictive diets, this diet doesn't recommend calorie counting. Instead, it allows kids to eat to their heart's content, provided they follow the cardinal principle of the keto diet: stick to high fat and low-carb foods. In this section, let's look at some of the helpful benefits of the keto diet for kids.

Weight Loss and Management

One of the popular reasons why people are attracted to the ketogenic diet is the weight loss benefits it offers. When you restrict carbs from your child's diet, all the excess sodium and water that's present in their body is eliminated. So, the initial weight loss comes from the loss of water weight. They will be encouraged to increase their intake of high-fat foods that further leads to weight loss. It's not just carbs that are reduced from their diet, but it also eliminates sugars and refined foods. Therefore, it gives them a steady supply of energy, and there will be no more sugar highs or energy crashes. Once their body gets used to this diet, they will feel energized throughout the day and will not experience any unpleasant energy fluctuations.

It is also believed that the human body takes longer to digest fats than carbs. The carbs your kid eats are readily transformed into energy. However, fats cannot be digested easily. Since they stay in the body for prolonged periods, they release energy slowly and steadily. This, in turn, will naturally reduce your child's urge to snack. Once the number of snacks they consume is reduced, it will naturally reduce their overall calorie intake. A combination of all these factors will lead to weight loss. Since childhood obesity is the major risk factor for various chronic health conditions, the first step is to tackle this condition. With the ketogenic diet, you can help your child attain and maintain their ideal weight.

Healthier Eating Habits

Most of us tend to form certain habits unknowingly and they are often formed in our childhood. The best time to learn something new is childhood. Think of a child's brain as a smartphone with limited storage. As the smartphone is used over the years, the storage space available in it usually reduces. This is one of the reasons why kids are adept at picking up new skills when compared to adults. If you want to teach your child some healthy eating habits, then start young. The habits your child learns in their childhood will stay with them all their life. Once they get used to a healthy eating pattern such as the one prescribed by the keto diet, they will get used to eating healthy and wholesome meals.

Improved Energy Levels

There are three macronutrients that your child's diet should include, and they are proteins, fats, and carbs. Each of these macros produces energy in one form or the other. Out of the lot, fat is the most energy-dense nutrient present. The human body obtains about 9 calories of energy from 1 g of fat and just about 4 calories of energy from 1 g of carbs or 1 g of proteins. Therefore, the largest energy store present in the human body is primarily composed of fat cells. So, once your child's body starts to burn fats, then it will keep providing plenty of energy to them unless they consume excessive carbs.

Absorption of Nutrients

Certain nutrients are not soluble in water. If your child's diet doesn't contain any healthy fats, then their body will not absorb these nutrients. For instance, fats are necessary to absorb essential nutrients such as vitamins A, vitamins E, vitamin D, vitamins K, and other carotenoids. If their diet doesn't have the necessary fats, then it can lead to a severe deficiency of all these vital nutrients. A deficiency of vitamin A leads to anemia, retardation of growth, and also increases their risk of infections. On the other hand, a deficiency of vitamin D reduces his bone density, causes bone weakness, and can even lead to bone deformities.

Reduces the Risk of Diseases

It is believed that the keto diet can reduce the risk of metabolic syndrome, Type II diabetes, obesity, dementia, bipolar disorder, certain types of cancers, Parkinson's, and even polycystic ovary syndrome. However, plenty of research is still required to formally determine whether the ketogenic diet can do all this or not. The keto diet has been proven to be a helpful means to regulate and control childhood obesity. Obesity is the precursor for a variety of chronic health conditions such as diabetes, cardiovascular disorders, and even digestive troubles. By controlling obesity, the keto diet offers your child a fair chance to reduce their risk of various other harmful health conditions.

Epilepsy Treatment

As mentioned in the previous chapter, the ketogenic diet was initially created as a treatment for epilepsy in children. Several studies show its effectiveness to treat and manage epileptic seizures in children. Unlike pharmaceutical drugs that bring along a spectrum of harmful side effects, the keto diet is a safe treatment option. Also, this diet is not just helpful for children, but adults too. You will find more supporting evidence about the keto diet as a treatment for epilepsy in the next section.

Science Supports the Keto Diet

It's a popular opinion that diets are not recommended for kids. However, this concept is only partially true. Yes, restrictive diets are bad for kids, but there are certain diets that are good for them, such as the ketogenic diet. In fact, when used for medical reasons, the ketogenic diet is quite helpful for a kid's health.

NOTE: Before you introduce this diet to your child's routine, seek a doctor's opinion. It is widely recommended that a child should not attempt this diet unless it is under medical supervision. As long as your child's doctor agrees to this course of treatment, you've nothing to worry about.

It's believed that the ketogenic diet is an incredibly effective tool for weight loss, not just for adults, but also for children. Since obesity is a rampant problem these days, the importance of a healthy diet cannot be overlooked.

In the *Journal of Pediatric Endocrinology and*

Metabolism, a study was published in the year 2012 that helped measure the weight loss effects of the ketogenic diet compared to those following a low-calorie diet. This study carefully observed the eating patterns of 58 obese children for six months. The children on the keto diet lost more weight, waist circumference, and fat mass when compared to kids on a low-calorie diet plan. It was also noted that there were significant improvements in the levels of fasting insulin in children who followed the ketogenic diet. Therefore, the researchers of the study concluded that the ketogenic diet was a safe and feasible alternative for weight loss in children.

In 2003, another study was conducted which carefully observed the effects of a low carb diet in overweight adolescents. This study was stretched over a period of 12 weeks, and the researchers noted that the children who followed a carb-restricted diet lost more weight than the ones who didn't. Also, the children who followed a low-carb diet had better cholesterol levels. So, the researchers of this study concluded that a low carb diet is an effective way to promote weight loss in overweight people and leads to fat loss without harming their overall lipid profile.

In 2010, another study was published which compared the results between a high-protein and low carb diet to a low-fat diet. 46 obese children were observed and half of them were prescribed a low carb diet, while the rest followed a low-fat diet. It was noted that the children who followed a high-protein and low carb diet lost more weight than others and they did not experience any harmful side effects. The researchers of this study concluded that a high-protein and low carb diet was a safe and effective alternative for weight loss in obese adolescents.

When the observations from all these studies are put together, it becomes fairly obvious that the keto diet is a brilliant dietary protocol that promotes healthy weight loss in children. Children can effectively say goodbye to childhood obesity with this diet.

Possible Side-Effects of the Keto Diet

Now that you're aware of all the different benefits offered by the ketogenic diet, it might sound quite perfect. However, even the ketogenic diet has certain side effects. These side effects might or might not occur. Whenever you make any dietary changes, your body needs time to adapt to the diet. So, when you try to transition your child from their regular diet to the ketogenic diet, their body will take time, too. While it gets used to this diet, your child might experience a couple of uncomfortable symptoms. Don't worry about these symptoms because they are usually quite mild. Also, they disappear as soon as your child's body gets used to the ketogenic diet. As mentioned in the previous chapters, the human body usually depends on glucose to provide energy. On the ketogenic diet, this source of energy shifts from glucose to fats. Therefore, it is obvious that his body will also need some time to get accustomed to the new dietary regimen.

It usually takes anywhere between 7-10 days to get used to the ketogenic diet. In the meanwhile, your child might experience some of the following symptoms.

The most common symptoms are fatigue, muscle cramps, headache, lack of motivation, sugar cravings, irritability, and nausea. All of these symptoms are collectively known as the keto flu. When your child's body shifts from a high carb to a low carb diet, it reduces their insulin levels. When these levels are low, the liver converts the available fat into ketones that are used instead of glucose. When their body uses ketones to provide energy, it is in a state of ketosis. It takes the brain and all the important organs in the body some time to get used to this new source of fuel. When the insulin levels decrease, his body's usual response is to remove any excess sodium from within. Due to this, your child can feel a little tired and irritable. You don't have to worry about these symptoms because they are often mild. Here are some simple tips that can be used to alleviate or avoid these symptoms altogether.

More Water

When your child's body tries to get used to using fats instead of glucose to provide energy, it loses a lot of water. Not just water, but it also expels all the sodium stored within. When this happens, your child can feel quite tired and irritated. Dehydration can also cause mood swings and headaches. Therefore, ensure that your child gets plenty of water, especially during the first week of the keto diet. Not just water, but also add a couple of electrolytes to their daily drinks. If their electrolyte levels are stable and their body is thoroughly hydrated, it helps reduce or even altogether avoid the symptoms of the keto flu. So, keep an eye on your child's water intake, and make it a point that they drink at least one glass of water with every meal they consume.

Slow Transition

Never be in a hurry, and certainly don't try to rush your child into this diet. Keep in mind that even if it doesn't seem like much to you, it is a major lifestyle change for your child. If their usual diet was rich in carbs, sugars, or other processed foods, it will take a while to get used to the new diet. A diet that's primarily composed of carbs and sugars is usually quite addictive. As with any addiction, it takes the body a while to get over it. So, be patient with your child and don't be in a hurry. Follow the simple tips discussed in the previous chapter to slowly transition them into this new diet. Even if it takes a couple of weeks to get them used to the diet, it's okay. Take about two weeks to get your child used to the idea of consuming high-fat and low carb meals before you jump into a full-fledged keto routine.

More Dietary Fats

Most of the side effects of the keto flu can be easily resolved when you increase your child's intake of salt and fluids. However, if they continue to experience any of the symptoms of the keto flu, increase their consumption of dietary fats. There is plenty of misconception about the nature of fat, and the role it plays in the body. We are all guilty of wrongly demonizing fats and all our fears are quite baseless. Yes, not all fats are equal and there are certain fats that are healthy. However, the keto diet encourages the consumption of healthy fats, which are good for your child's health. If you restrict their intake of fats while cutting down on their intake of carbs, it will quickly lead to starvation. Therefore, don't make this mistake, and let your child eat plenty of dietary fats.

Note: If the symptoms persist, seek medical attention immediately and stop the diet.

Get Some Rest

While their body gets used to the new diet, their energy levels can fluctuate a little. Once their body starts to continuously burn fat to provide energy, they will not experience any oscillations in their overall energy levels. In the meanwhile, it is your responsibility to ensure that they get plenty of rest. Don't allow them to exert themselves, and certainly don't push them into vigorous physical activities. Allow them to play, but monitor their overall activity levels. Once the body is used to this diet, which is usually after a week or so, it allows them to get back to their previous routine.

If you are worried about any of the possible side effects of the ketogenic diet, ensure that you consult your child's pediatrician immediately. In fact, make it a point that you consult your child's healthcare provider before you make any dietary changes. Another important point you must keep in mind is that these side effects might not even show up. The different symptoms discussed in this section are merely the probable side effects of the ketogenic diet. Your child might or might not experience the symptoms. Regardless of all this, ensure that you give your child sufficient dietary fats, keep their body hydrated, and get sufficient rest to make the transition easier. Once their body is accustomed to the keto diet, it will constantly burn fats to give their body a steady flow of energy.

A Conversation About Nutrition

Children are almost like sponges; they soak in everything that happens around them. They mimic actions that they observe, repeat the words they hear from others, and even follow the behavioral patterns they see others present around them. Parents obviously play a very important role in a child's life. In fact, parents are one of the first influencers a child meets. As a parent, it is your job to model healthy behaviors you want your child to follow. However, we live in a society that actively indulges in body shaming, supports fad diets, and promotes the idea of perfection. When all these things are put together, it is no wonder that children tend to develop eating disorders, form unhealthy relationships with food, or don't view food in a positive way.

It is saddening to note that in the last couple of decades, the rates of childhood obesity have almost tripled and it has become a very big problem these days. Instead of sharing home-cooked meals, ordering food, depending on fast food, or even ready to eat meals has become increasingly popular. Also, more and more children and young adults try different fad diets to promote weight loss. Eating disorders and childhood obesity are not only dangerous for your child's well-being, but they also encourage an unhealthy relationship with food. All these factors will have a negative effect on your child's life sooner or later. Therefore, as a parent, it is your responsibility to ensure that your child keeps an open mind to food and doesn't label food as either good or bad. So, be mindful of your behavior around your child and have an open conversation about nutrition with them. This conversation needs to be modified according to their age and mindset. If you don't know where to begin, here are a few tips that will come in handy.

Keep Trying

At times, you might need to introduce the same food item to your child a couple of times before they like it. Usually, a child's tastes tend to change and develop with time. So, don't be disheartened if they don't like olives or anchovies the first time they eat them. After a while, he will certainly come around. In the meanwhile, try to cook using different techniques. If one technique doesn't work, try another one, and something or the other will click. Keep trying and get a little creative.

Don't Label Food

Usually, parents tend to label food as either good or bad. For instance, most of us label all junk food as bad and fresh fruits and vegetables as good food. When you do this, it tends to create a rather judgmental image of food in your child's mind. Of course, it is not healthy to allow your child to eat a pint of ice cream, but it is important that you teach them about foods that are important for their health. All snacks can be fun foods that your child can eat once in a while. When you label foods, your child tends to develop a negative relationship with it. For instance, they will feel guilty whenever they eat the so-called unhealthy junk food.

Educate Your Child

Instead of concentrating on weight and body image, try to educate your child about making healthy choices in life. Usually, children who are overweight or obese are often ridiculed. However, excessive weight gain in childhood often results in chronic health conditions later in life. Instead of stressing on weight loss, try to teach your child the importance of making healthy choices. Introduce a healthy lifestyle to your child that includes a healthy diet, plenty of exercise, and a constructive coping mechanism.

Identify Hunger

A lot of parents force their kids to eat at specific times regardless of whether their child is hungry or not. If your family dinnertime is at 8 p.m, then ensure that your child eats something at that time. However, don't force them to eat a heavy meal if they aren't hungry. At the same time, don't encourage them to eat later. After a while, their body will get used to the specific eating schedule. Whenever your child feels like eating, ask them to identify whether they are hungry or if it is something else that makes them want to eat. Ask them to check in with their emotions and identify hunger.

Ditch Unnecessary Rules

Allow your child to understand when their tummy is full. Never push them to eat more than what their body needs. As babies, we all know how much we need to eat, and when we're hungry. However, as we grow older, we lose a sense of this feeling. So, when your child says they feel full, don't force them to eat. As a parent, you merely need to provide nutritious meals to them and ensure that they eat appropriate portions. Don't serve your kid an adult-sized portion and expect them to finish it.

Body Positivity

Nobody is perfect, and bodies come in different sizes and shapes. Therefore, body shaming must be banned, and instead body-positive language should be used. So, be mindful of how you talk about yourself and others when you are in the presence of your child. Not just that, but also ensure that you don't criticize yourself unnecessarily. Before you can teach your child behavior, you need to follow the same. To do this, you need to accept certain things about yourself. Once you accept your body the way it is, in spite of its imperfections, you will feel better about yourself. This is the kind of body positivity you should share with your child. Be mindful to not criticize your body or others' bodies in front of your child, and never teach them that exercising is about weight loss. Instead, encourage them to exercise because it is a fun way to keep their body healthy.

Now that you're aware of the different things you need to talk to your child about, try to work on it immediately. Usually, children tend to learn these things from the adults around them, their friends, or anyone else they interact with. Since most kids these days have easy access to the Internet, they tend to pick up all sorts of wrong messages from it. So, it is time to step in and take the responsibility to change your child's life for the better.

4

PROPER MEAL PREP FOR KIDS ON KETO

Keto-Friendly Foods

The ketogenic diet isn't necessarily restrictive. It merely depends on how creative you can get with the various ingredients available. There are plenty of low carb alternatives to naturally starchy foods. In this section, let's look at all the different foods that your child can consume while on this diet.

Healthy Fats

Anywhere between 70 and 75% of your child's daily calorie intake will be in the form of naturally fatty foods. Most fats are derived from natural sources such as meats, nuts, and healthy oils. Monounsaturated and saturated fats, especially the ones derived from grass-fed sources, should be added to your child's keto diet. The various types of fats and oils you can include are avocados, fatty fish, unprocessed animal fats, lard, egg yolks, grass-fed butter, coconut butter, Brazil nuts, cocoa butter, coconut oil, avocado oil, macadamia oil, extra virgin olive oil, and avocados.

Proteins

Proteins must account for anywhere between 15

and 20% of your child's daily calorie intake. When you purchase meats and proteins, opt for the grass-fed varieties whenever possible instead of the factory-farmed variants. The various sources of protein you can include are pork (pork chops, ground pork, unprocessed bacon, and unglazed ham), beef (steak, ribs, and ground beef), seafood (anchovies, sardines, salmon, caviar, tuna, mackerel, shrimp, lobster, crabs, and other shellfish), poultry (chicken, turkey, and any other poultry meats), whole eggs, tofu, natto, spirulina, tempeh, and nutritional yeast.

Vegetables

Reduce your child's intake of starchy vegetables such as root vegetables. A major chunk of the calories they consume from carbs should come from low carb vegetables. There are a variety of vegetables you can include as long as they grow above ground. Some of the healthy examples of low carb vegetables include mushrooms, bell peppers, watercress, bok choy, Pak Choi, Swiss chard, spinach, amaranth, kale, water chestnuts, lettuce, beansprouts, okra, sugar snap peas, bamboo shoots, nori, spaghetti squash, celery, zucchini, radish, pumpkin, green beans, fennel, cucumbers, eggplants, cauliflower, cabbage, brussels sprouts, broccoli, arugula, asparagus, and artic1hokes.

Tip: As long as it grows above ground, it is usually low-carb. Don't forget to include plenty of green vegetables in your child's diet. They are rich in vitamins and essential nutrients but are low in carbs.

Fruits

All low-glycemic fruits are permitted on the keto diet in regulated quantities. If you aren't careful, the carbs and sugars in fruits can quickly add up, and remove your child's body from ketosis. To avoid all this, pay attention to all the fruits they consume. The different fruits you can include are avocados, blackberries, blueberries, olives, raspberries, strawberries, cranberries, mulberries, cherries, lemons, limes, tomatoes, coconut, and cantaloupes.

Dairy Products

When it comes to dairy products, don't hesitate to choose the full-fat dairy products. Let go of any misconceptions you have about full-fat dairy products being bad for your child's health. These foods are rich in dietary fats and essential nutrients that are good for their health. Instead of low-fat and low-calorie options, which contain added sugars, opt for full-fat variants. The different dairy products you can add are butter, milk, cream, soft cheeses, hard cheeses, cream cheese, feta, Greek yogurt, sour cream, ghee, and unsweetened heavy whipping cream.

Nuts and Seeds

Nuts and seeds are excellent sources of vital nutrients and healthy dietary fats. However, they should be consumed only in moderation. A small handful of nuts and seeds can make for a filling and a healthy snack. However, don't add too many nuts to your child's diet because there can be some carbs in them. The nuts and seeds you can add are almonds, hazelnuts, pecans, walnuts, pine nuts, Brazil nuts, macadamia nuts, pumpkin seeds, sunflower seeds, sesame seeds, flax seeds, and hemp seeds. Aside from nuts and seeds, you can also use butters and flours made from them. Avoid peanuts since they are legumes and are rich in carbs.

Herbs, Spices, and Condiments

All spices and herbs can be easily added to the diet. They can be used to lend additional flavors, and alleviate the flavor profile of a regular meal. You don't have to hesitate and you certainly don't have to hold back. Most processed condiments contain some form of sugars and carbs in them. So, always read the list of ingredients before you add anything to your shopping cart. For instance, tomato ketchup and barbecue sauce have artificial sweeteners and sugars in them.

Beverages

All prepackaged beverages such as fruit juices and sodas aren't allowed. Ensure that your child drinks plenty of water while on the ketogenic diet. You can spruce up water with some mint leaves, berries, or even slices of lemon.

Foods to Avoid

Now that you're aware of the different keto foods you can include, let's look at the ones you should stay away from. Most of the foods discussed in this section are filled with empty calories. It essentially means they give your child plenty of calories but they are devoid of any useful nutrients. Also, they are rich in carbs, unhealthy sugars, and processed oils. Whenever you shop for groceries, avoid all these items.

Fruits

It might be surprising to see fruits included in the category of foods to be avoided. The keto diet restricts the consumption of fruits rich in carbs and sugars. The different fruits your child must stay away from are oranges, pineapples, bananas, apples, grapes, mangoes, tangerines, pears, nectarines, peaches, and pre-processed fruit juices. Even if a smoothie includes any of these sugar-rich fruits, it is excluded from the ketogenic diet. Apart from regular fruits, avoid dried fruits such as dried mangoes, raisins, and dates. Whenever you purchase any frozen produce, read through the list of ingredients. At times, frozen fruits are artificially sweetened and they have some hidden carbs.

Vegetables

As a rule of thumb, the keto diet suggests that all vegetables that grow beneath the ground need to be avoided. The vegetables that contain more carbs have a high starch count. The different vegetables you need to avoid include sweet potatoes, potatoes, peas, yams, parsnips, artichokes, and cassava. Whenever you purchase any prepackaged foods, ensure that you carefully look for these ingredients. Any food item with these ingredients is prohibited on the ketogenic diet.

Grains

The one principle of the keto diet you must always follow is to reduce your carb intake and increase the consumption of healthy fats. Grains are normally filled with plenty of carbs that can halt ketosis in your child's body. Make it a point to avoid giving him grains in any form as much as you possibly can. The most common grains you need to avoid are oats, oatmeal, wheat, sourdough, barley, quinoa, rice, sorghum, corn, buckwheat, rye, white or processed flour, pumpernickel, and so on. In addition to the grains, avoid products (pasta, pizza, bread, cookies, etc.) and flours made with these grains, too.

Legumes

Legumes such as beans and peas are filled with proteins and various other helpful nutrients. However, they also have plenty of carbs in them. Therefore, the different types of legumes that need to be avoided on the ketogenic diet are green peas, navy beans, cannellini beans, kidney beans, black beans, black-eyed peas, lentils, chickpeas, lima beans, pinto beans, and great northern beans.

Protein

To help your child maintain and develop chest muscle mass, ensure that they consume sufficient protein. The two best sources of proteins which are low in carbs are poultry and naturally fatty fish. You can easily include fattier cuts of meat, such as fatty fish, ribeye steaks, or even chicken thighs without any hesitation. Plenty of meats and animal products can be added, but processed meats should be avoided at all costs. Most processed meats such as deli meats are quite tasty, but they have carbs and sugars in them. This, coupled with all the added preservatives that promote its shelf life, aren't good for your child's health. So, avoid bacon that has any added sugar, processed meats (sausages, pepperoni, hot dogs, prosciutto, or salami), and breaded meats.

Dairy Products

Dairy products are usually low in carbs and are healthy, but in moderation. The most common dairy products you must eliminate from your child's diet are the ones labeled as low-fat, fat-free, zero-fat, or diet. To compensate for their low fat content, these products usually include carbs. The common dairy foods you need to avoid are condensed milk, fat-free or low-fat yogurt, sweetened and flavored milk or yogurt, skimmed milk and low-fat milk, and creamed cottage cheese.

Unhealthy Fats

All fats are not created equally, and certain fats can wreak havoc on your child's health. The keto diet is a high-fat diet, but it encourages the intake of healthy fats and actively discourages the consumption of any unhealthy ones. Any oils or fats that contain trans fats are bad for your kid's health. Avoid any hydrogenated vegetable oils, trans fats, and omega-6 fatty acids. Whenever you cook, ensure that oils don't reach extremely high temperatures and use walnut or sesame oil only for salad dressings, but not for cooking. Avoid processed fats, polyunsaturated fats, and trans fats, such as margarine and hydrogenated oils.

Beverages

You must pay attention to whatever your child drinks. Most beverages are rich sources of hidden sugars and carbs. Most of your child's liquid consumption should be in the form of water. Always encourage them to drink plenty of water. The different beverages your child needs to avoid are hot chocolate, sodas, root beer, ginger ale, carbonated drinks, energy drinks, tonic water, vitamin waters, sports drinks, prepackaged fruit juices, and anything that contains sugars. If you want your child to drink juices, ensure that you make them at home and don't purchase any pre-packaged fruit juices.

There are plenty of hidden carbs in most of the preprocessed drinks available on the market these days. These hidden sugars and carbs can quickly add up and wreak havoc on your child's health. When in doubt about a specific food item, use this simple test: if it looks like it was mass-produced or manufactured in a factory, then avoid it as much as you can. Also, don't forget to carefully read through the list of ingredients. If you don't recognize any of the ingredients used or cannot understand them, avoid such products. Try to limit your child's intake of processed foods and replace them with natural foods.

Keto Meal Prep Tips

Meal prep is quite simple, and it helps save plenty of time during busy weekdays. Meal prep, as the name suggests, is all about prepping for a meal. It is about dedicating some time to batch cook specific ingredients, prepare full meals, or partially prepare meals for the upcoming week. If you want your child to get all the nourishment their body needs, then they need to eat healthy meals. When you have time, it is quite easy to cook elaborate meals. However, you probably wouldn't have the energy to cook meals all the time, especially if you've had an extremely busy or tiring day. In such instances, meal prepping certainly helps make things easier.

Take a moment and think about the situation. Why do most parents let their children eat junk food? It is readily available and takes no effort. If you had some protein and sauce stored in the fridge, how difficult would it be to cook? For instance, if you had a batch of meatballs and tomato sauce in the fridge, it won't take long to make spaghetti and meatballs. That is what meal prep is about. It could be something as simple as cutting and chopping vegetables, portioning the ingredients for different meals, or even batch cooking certain sauces, soups, and curries. Ideally, over the weekend, dedicate a couple of hours for meal prep, and cooking during the week will become very simple and easy.

With meal prep, you will realize that it becomes incredibly easy to feed your family delicious and nutritious meals without spending hours in the kitchen. Meal prep also allows you to plan meals for the upcoming week. So, when you are aware of the meals you have to cook, it becomes easier to make a list of all the ingredients you require. Therefore, meal prep, not only saves you time and effort, but it also helps with grocery shopping. Apart from all this, with meal prep, you can ensure that you and your family eat healthy foods that are keto-friendly. If you want to become good at meal prep, here are some practical and simple tips that will come in handy.

Plan for the Week

Before you can do some meal prep, you need to think about the different meals you wish to cook. Whenever you know what you need to cook, it becomes easier to cook and it reduces time waste. While you plan the meals for a week, ensure that you consider your little one. Go through the different recipes given in this book, and ask your child what they would like to eat. The simplest way to plan for a week is to maintain a journal. Write down the three different meals you need to cook every day, and don't forget to include a couple of simple snacks. Pick a recipe you'd want to cook and make a note of it against the respective day. Once you are aware of the different meals you need to cook, you can easily come up with a grocery list. So, before you can meal prep, ensure that your pantry is well stocked and you have all the keto-friendly ingredients you need.

Make Some Time

If you want meal prep to work, you need to have the time to cook. Usually, weekends are ideal for meal prep. If you know you will be free on a specific day, every week, ensure that you dedicate at least 3 to 4 hours for meal prepping. Now that you have all the ingredients on hand, it is time to meal prep.

Double the Portions

Go through the different recipes you wish to cook and make note of the ones you can batch cook. The great thing about meal prepping is that it allows you to cook large portions of certain recipes. So, if you know Bolognese sauce is a family favorite, then cook a couple of extra portions and freeze it. The days when you have no energy to cook, you merely need to reheat the sauce and serve it with a salad or zucchini noodles!

Proper Containers

Ensure that you have proper containers to store your prepped meals. If you want, you can portion certain ingredients and store them in individual containers. Use freezer-friendly containers and don't forget to use baggies or freezer safe ziploc bags. An example of something good for freezing is smoothies. Smoothies are an incredible snack and they are quite filling. In fact, smoothies can be served as breakfast, too. If you wish to include smoothies, then collect all the ingredients, divide them into individual servings, and place them in airtight freezer bags.

Overlapping Ingredients

When you pick any recipes for meal prep, try to group them based on certain overlapping ingredients. For instance, if you need zucchini noodles for a curry dish, you can repurpose them for a stir-fry some other night. Grilled vegetables can also be served as a side or even turned into a simple casserole.

Frozen Food

Don't shy away from frozen food, and instead, embrace it with open arms. Frozen vegetables and fruits will make your life easier when it comes to meal prep. You merely need to thaw them and use them in regular cooking. Since most frozen foods are partially cooked, it reduces the overall cooking time, too. Frozen vegetables have the same nutritional value as fresh produce, so you have nothing to worry about. Also, frozen produce is often cheaper than fresh varieties.

Include a Variety

If you want your child to get excited about their new diet, then ensure that there is plenty of variety. It is quite boring if you have to eat the same meal over and over again. Therefore, add several types of dishes, and try to mix and match various ingredients to create different meals. For example, if you make a couple of different sauces, you can use them to make different recipes. Make a note of any sauces you can cook, batch cook them, and store them in the fridge.

Prep the Protein

When it comes to the keto diet, there is plenty of fatty protein to choose from. From seafood to meat and poultry, there is a wide variety. Once you are aware of the different meals you wish to cook, it is time to prep the protein. Ensure that your child gets at least 70 to 75% of their daily calorie needs from naturally fatty sources such as seafood, meats, and poultry. You can grill, braise, or even roast some proteins and store them for later.

Prep Low-carb Vegetables

Don't forget to prep different low carb vegetables. Ensure that your child gets most of their daily carbs from low carb vegetables, instead of grains or any other source. So, you can dice, chop, cut, grill, roast, or even steamed vegetables, and store them for later. Once you prep the low carb vegetables, cooking with them becomes incredibly easy.

Use the different tips discussed in this section, and cooking will become quite easy. You don't have to spend hours in the kitchen every day to cook healthy meals. Prepping not only reduces the overall cooking time, but it also ensures that your child gets their daily nourishment in the form of delicious and healthy keto-friendly meals.

Transition to Keto Diet

When you are aware of all the undesirable foods present in your child's diet, you might be quite tempted to get rid of all processed foods. However, if you make any drastic changes, it will not do your child any good. Instead, your child might feel frustrated, confused and angry that they don't get to eat the foods they enjoy.

While it is up to you to ensure your child eats

healthy meals, you also need to remember that the process of properly introducing a diet also lies on your shoulders. How you introduce a diet and enforce its rules will dictate the relationship your child shares with food. For instance, if you shame them whenever they eat unhealthy foods or punish them, they will develop an unhealthy relationship with food. They might either loathe some foods or even hide their eating patterns from you. Neither of these things is desirable for your child's overall health and well-being. Even if you have their best intentions at heart, you should introduce the diet to them in phases. Ensure that they slowly transition from their regular eating habits to the keto diet.

In some instances, going cold turkey might work, but if you want to change your child's eating habits, you must be sensitive to their needs. They probably wouldn't understand why their favorite sugary treats have disappeared from the usual meals. Therefore, you cannot make this change overnight.

Instead, you should slowly and gradually introduce the new pattern of eating to them. The best way to start this is to eliminate an item or two from their usual meal. Instead of prepackaged or processed fruit juices, you can replace these with water. Or, perhaps you can replace the sugary cereals your child has in the morning with healthier alternatives such as eggs for breakfast! Depending on how acclimatized your child was to their sugary drinks or cereals, it can take between a week and 10 days to implement this change. Regardless of how they behave, you need to persevere if you want to make this change stick. In fact, don't be surprised if your child resists the first time you replace sugary fruit juice with a glass of water. It might happen a couple of times, but after that, even your child will soon get used to it.

Once you reduce the more obvious sugar and carb-rich junk food such as cookies, chips, chocolates, sweets, or any other unhealthy foods, it is time to slowly reduce their carb intake. This means you need to slowly cut down on the amount of pasta, bread, or rice they eat. Don't eliminate these starchy foods from their diet immediately. Instead, slowly reduce the number of undesirable starches and increase their intake of other foods. For instance, if your child loves spaghetti and meatballs, serve them more meatballs and slowly reduce the amount of spaghetti they eat. This way, they will not feel deprived of the food they love and at the same time, you get the satisfaction that they are eating healthier meals. Pay attention to your child's immediate reaction when you introduce this change. They might ask you for more spaghetti, but tell them they can eat more once they eat more of the other items on the plate. Chances are that by the time they do this, they won't be hungry for anything else.

It might be a little difficult at first. In fact, prepare yourself for some resistance and tantrums. However, remind yourself of the long-term benefits your child stands to gain from the keto diet! This will certainly give you the motivation to persevere while you try to change your child's eating patterns. You can slowly introduce and eliminate certain foods from your child's diet. Here are a couple of more steps you can use to make this transition easier.

Say Goodbye to Bread

Processed flour, and especially white flour, is bad for one's health. White flour and all products made from it are undesirable for your child's overall well-being. Unfortunately, bread is a major food group for most children these days. The usual white bread is incredibly unhealthy and barely has any nutritional value in it. The simplest way to eliminate unhealthy carbs from your child's diet is to say bye-bye to bread. Once again, it is important that this change is gradual. Here is an easy tip you should follow: start "bread-free" days. If you want, you can swap bread for a wrap or maybe a thinner loaf. Apart from this, there are plenty of keto-friendly flours you can use to bake bread! Instead of traditional sandwiches, why don't you replace them with a lettuce wrap or whole grain flatbread?

Keep Things Simple

A common mistake most parents make when they try to get their kids to eat healthier is they make things complicated. Don't do this; keep things simple. It might be quite tempting to cook elaborate meals to compensate for the absence of carbs in your child's diet. However, this practice is certainly not sustainable in the long run. There will be days when you cannot cook elaborate meals and if they get used to it, they will always expect it. Apart from this, all the extra pressure to cook elaborate meals can stress you out and force you to go back to the old ways.

The simplest way to start this is with breakfast. Instead of the processed cereals your child eats, replace them with something as simple as a bowl of yogurt and some fruits, or maybe even make a breakfast smoothie. On weekends, you can treat them to snazzy omelets or something else. This simple practice will make the weekend seem like a special occasion to them, it reduces the daily stress of cooking, and it ensures that your child eats healthy meals throughout the week. If your child refuses to let go of cereal, don't forget to negotiate with them. You don't have to necessarily give in to their tantrums or demands, but you can offer cereal as a special treat. Allow them to eat cereal once in a while, but don't replace the boxes once they eat their way through them.

Involve Your Kid

Most adults don't really give their kids sufficient

credit. Your child might not notice the subtle changes to their diet initially, but eventually, they will and might resist or even revolt. To avoid all this, involve your child from the beginning. If they are old enough, you can easily explain the importance of healthier eating habits to them. Don't keep them in the dark and try to engage them as much as you possibly can when it comes to the new diet. Whenever you plan the meals, ask them what they would like to eat. Ask them for their opinions, input, and suggestions. If they don't want to eat something, ask them what alternative they would want to eat. You can get them involved with food prep and grocery shopping. This is a great way in which you can bond with your child and make them feel more involved in their life. It will also give your child a sense of control. When they know that you are giving them certain responsibilities, they will feel better about themselves.

Organization Matters

Unfortunately, one of the primary reasons why children depend on junk food is because it is readily available, and convenient. Prepackaged food, processed food, and ready meals are easy to prepare. Parents usually resort to these meals because, after a long or tiring day, they have little or no time to cook meals. It is highly unrealistic to assume that every parent has the same amount of time or energy to cook healthy meals from scratch. Don't set such unrealistic goals for yourself. Instead, learn to make things more manageable. Try to get your routine as organized as possible. Over the weekend, you can do some basic meal prep for the upcoming week. Ensure that your pantry is fully stocked with all keto-friendly ingredients. When all the supplies you need are readily available and some meal prep is done, it becomes incredibly easy to whip up healthy meals during the week.

Deal with Picky Eating

If a child doesn't eat certain things, parents usually assume that their child is a picky eater. In reality, the child might simply be seeking the parent's attention. Use a plate with compartments and turn eating into a game. Or, perhaps you can offer more variety and include several small portions of vegetables, dairy, meat or fish instead of carbs. A common mistake that parents make is that once they realize their child as a picky eater, they let them eat whatever they want as long as they eat something. Don't make this mistake, or it will spoil the relationship your child has with food. Avoid labelling your child as a picky eater and certainly don't allow them to get away with whatever they want.

If your child doesn't eat properly at one meal, don't offer them snacks before the next meal. If you do this, in the long run, your child will become so dependent on the snacks that they wouldn't want to eat proper meals. Avoid quick fixes and encourage your child to wait for their next meal. So, when they are hungry, they will eat whatever you serve. Usually, for picky eaters, the issue is mostly about being in control. The simplest way to tackle this situation is to get your child as involved in the cooking activities as possible.

5

KETOGENIC BREAKFAST RECIPES FOR KIDS

Cinnamon Roll Smoothie

Number of servings: 2

Preparation time: 5 minutes

Cooking time: 0 minute

Ingredients:

- 3 cups almond milk
- 1 teaspoon cinnamon powder
- 4 tablespoons vanilla protein powder
- 2 teaspoons flax meal
- 1/2 teaspoon vanilla extract
- Stevia drops to taste
- Ice as required

Directions:

1. Add almond milk, cinnamon, vanilla protein powder, flax meal, vanilla, stevia drops and ice into a blender.
2. Blend until it gets the right consistency.
3. Pour into 2 glasses and serve.

Make Ahead Sausage McMuffin

Number of servings: 6

Preparation time: 25 minutes

Cooking time: 40 minutes

Ingredients:

For sandwich filling:

- 6 chicken sausage links (3.5 ounces each)
- ½ cup grated sharp cheddar cheese
- Kosher salt to taste
- 10 eggs
- 2 teaspoons avocado oil or any other oil of your choice, per sausage link
- Freshly cracked pepper to taste

For biscuits:

- 4 cups almond flour
- 1 teaspoon garlic powder
- 1 teaspoon onion powder
- Freshly cracked pepper to taste
- 1 cup melted butter
- 4 teaspoons baking powder
- 1 teaspoon salt, preferably kosher
- 4 eggs, beaten

Directions:

To make biscuits:

1. Sift almond flour into a large mixing bowl. Stir in the salt, onion powder, pepper and garlic powder.
2. Add eggs into another bowl and whisk well. Whisk in the melted butter.
3. Now pour the egg mixture into the bowl of almond flour and stir with a spatula until well incorporated.
4. Place a sheet of parchment paper on each of 2 large baking sheets. Divide the dough into 16 equal portions and shape into biscuits.

Place the biscuits on the prepared baking sheet. Leave sufficient gap between the biscuits.
5. Sprinkle cracked pepper on top of the biscuits.
6. Preheat the oven to 350° F.
7. Place the baking sheet in the oven. Set the timer for about 15 to 16 minutes. When the biscuits are ready, they should be golden brown on top. Bake for longer if required.
8. Remove the sheet from the oven and let it cool.
9. Bake the remaining biscuits in a similar manner. You will need 2 biscuits per sandwich. Store the remaining biscuits in an airtight container in the refrigerator. They can last for 5 – 7 days. You can use them in some other recipes as well.

<u>To make eggs:</u>

1. Add eggs into a bowl and whisk until nice and frothy.
2. Add salt and pepper to taste and whisk well.
3. Place a large, nonstick, ovenproof pan over

medium heat. Add oil and swirl the pan so that the oil spreads all over the pan.
4. Pour the egg mixture into the pan and swirl the pan so that it spreads evenly. Once the eggs begin to set, turn off the heat.
5. Preheat the oven to 350° F.
6. Transfer the pan to the oven and bake for about 6 – 7 minutes or until set.
7. Loosen the egg and invert it onto your cutting board. Cut it into several rounds using a cookie cutter that is nearly the size of the biscuits. You should get 6 rounds in all. Transfer them to an airtight jar and refrigerate them. You should consume all within 3 days. To make them last longer, place them in the freezer.

On the day of serving

1. Take out a chicken sausage (use more if there are others in your family who are on keto diet- 1 sausage link per serving) and discard the casing. Shape into a patty.
2. Place a pan over medium-high flame. If you have a cast iron pan, these works best. Add

oil and when the oil heats, place the patty on the pan and cook until the underside is golden brown.
3. Flip sides and reduce the flame to medium heat. Sprinkle some cheese on the patty. Cover the pan with a lid and cook for about 3 minutes or until the underside is golden brown.
4. Remove the patty and place it on a plate.

To assemble:

1. Place a biscuit on a serving plate, with the flat side facing up. Place a patty over the biscuit. Place an egg round over the patty. Cover with another biscuit, flat side touching the egg.
2. The McMuffin is ready.

Keto Bread

Number of servings: 6

Preparation time: 30 minutes

Cooking time: 3 minutes

Ingredients:

For keto bread:

- 3.4 ounces almond flour
- 0.6 ounce whey protein isolate
- 1 teaspoon xanthan gum
- 1.5 ounces golden flaxseed meal
- 1 ½ teaspoons baking powder
- ½ teaspoon kosher salt
- 4 – 10 teaspoons erythritol or xylitol, to taste
- 2 ounces butter, melted, cooled
- 2 eggs
- 1 teaspoon apple cider vinegar
- 2 ounces sour cream or heavy cream

Directions:

1. Add all the dry ingredients into a bowl (almond flour, whey protein powder, xanthan gum, flaxseed meal, baking powder and salt). Stir well.
2. Whisk together eggs and erythritol in a mixing bowl using an electric hand mixer until pale in color.

3. With the hand mixer running, whisk in the melted butter and apple cider vinegar.
4. Add ¼ of the dry ingredients mixture and ¼ of the sour cream and whisk until well combined.
5. Repeat the previous step until all of it is added. You will have a very thick batter.
6. Pour the batter into 6 ramekins. Place the ramekins in the microwave and cook on high for 1½ minutes. You can also pour the batter into a larger microwave safe container and cook it. But, you will need to increase the cooking time to 2 ½ minutes.
7. Remove the ramekins/bowl from the microwave and let cool. Remove the bread from the ramekins. Cut the bread into slices if you are using a larger container for cooking. Cool for a few minutes.
8. You can use the bread now. It is best to use the bread while it is warm. You can also place the bread in an airtight container in the refrigerator. It can last for 3 – 4 days. You can use this bread in some other recipes as well.

Keto French Toast

Number of servings: 6

Preparation time: 15 minutes

Cooking time: 3 minutes

Ingredients:

For French toast:

- 6 slices keto bread (refer to the previous recipe)
- 2 tablespoons almond milk
- 1 teaspoon pure vanilla extract
- 2 tablespoons golden erythritol

- Unsalted, grass-fed butter, as required to cook
- 2 eggs
- 2 tablespoons heavy cream
- 1/8 teaspoon kosher salt
- 1 teaspoon ground cinnamon

To serve: Optional, use any 1 or more

- Sugar-free maple syrup
- A handful fresh berries
- Sugar-free salted caramel
- Any other keto-friendly toppings

Directions:

To make French toast:

1. Cut the bread into slices.
2. Add eggs, heavy cream, salt, almond milk and vanilla extract into a bowl and whisk well.
3. Add cinnamon and sweetener in another bowl and stir.
4. Place a pan over medium-high heat. Add about a tablespoon of butter and allow it to melt.

5. Dip a slice or 2 of the bread in the egg mixture for a couple of minutes. Remove the bread slice from the mixture. Shake off excess mixture and place the slice on the heated pan. Cook until the underside is golden brown.
6. Flip sides and cook the other side until golden brown. Remove with a spatula and place on a plate. Dust with cinnamon sugar.
7. Repeat the steps 2 - 6 and make the remaining French toast similarly.
8. Serve with toppings of your choice.

Variations in French toast: These are great ideas to serve the same thing in a different manner to your kid.

French toast balls:

1. Cut the bread into small cubes. Add the cubes into the egg mixture (step 10) and stir well. Add the cinnamon sugar and mix well.
2. Grease a muffin pan with some butter. Divide the mixture into muffin pans.
3. Set the temperature of the oven to 350° F and let it preheat.
4. Place the muffin tin in the oven. Set the

timer for about 15 to 20 minutes or until golden brown. Remove the muffin pan from the oven and let it cool for 5 minutes.
5. Run a knife around the edges of the balls, to loosen. Drizzle sugar-free syrup of your choice on top and serve.

Fried French toast:

1. Place a deep pan over medium heat. Let the oil heat.
2. Meanwhile, soak a few of the bread slices in the egg mixture (step 10) for 2 – 3 minutes.
3. When the oil is well heated, but not smoking, carefully drop the soaked bread slices in the hot oil. Fry until crunchy and golden brown all over.
4. Remove and set it aside. Sprinkle cinnamon sugar on top. Serve garnished with a slice of strawberry.

Stuffed French toast:

1. For this you need to make larger bread. Cut the bread into 3 inch thick slices. Discard the crust. Make a slit in each of the pieces, like a

pocket. Place some stuffing in the pocket, like Nutella (recipe given in pancake recipe).
2. Spoon the filling inside the pocket. You can also make a Nutella sandwich if you are not able to make pockets.
3. Place a pan over medium-high heat. Add about a tablespoon of butter and allow it to melt.
4. Dip a slice or 2 of the bread in the egg mixture for a couple of minutes. Remove the bread slice from the mixture. Shaking off excess mixture, place the slice on the heated pan. Cook until the underside is golden brown.
5. Flip sides and cook the other side until golden brown. Remove with a spatula and place on a plate. There is no need to dust cinnamon sugar, as Nutella is sweet.

French toast Roll-ups

1. Here again you need to make larger bread. Cut the bread into slices. Discard the crust. Place the slices on your countertop and roll the slices using a rolling pin.
2. Spread the filling of your choice. For

example, you can use cream cheese and thin strawberry slices. Place strawberry slices on the edges. Roll the bread along with the filling and place with its seam side facing down on a plate.
3. Follow steps 2 - 6 from the first French toast recipe and dip the roll instead of slice.

No-tatoes Bubble 'n' Squeak

Number of servings: 6

Preparation time: 15 minutes

Cooking time: About 20 minutes

Ingredients:

For mashed cauliflower:

- 1 medium cauliflower, chopped into florets
- 2 tablespoons butter
- 4 tablespoons heavy whipping cream
- Salt to taste
- ½ cup mozzarella, grated
- Pepper to taste

For No-tatoes Bubble 'n' squeak:

- 6 slices bacon, diced
- 1 medium onion, diced
- 2 green onions, sliced
- 4 tablespoons duck fat
- ½ cup grated Parmesan
- 2 teaspoons minced garlic
- 2 tablespoons butter
- 2 leeks, sliced
- 3.5 ounces Brussels sprouts, chopped

Directions:

To make mashed cauliflower:

1. If you have leftover mashed cauliflower, you can use this instead of making it from scratch. If not, add cauliflower, butter, and cream into a microwave safe bowl.
2. Microwave on high for 8 minutes, without covering. Stir the contents and cook for 4 more minutes. Stir once again. If the cauliflower is not cooked well, cook for another minute or so. It should be very soft.
3. Add salt and pepper to taste. Mash the cauliflower with a potato masher or use an immersion blender and blend until smooth.
4. Stir in the mozzarella cheese. Let it cool.

To make Bubble and Squeak:

1. Place a skillet over medium-high flame. Add bacon and cook until crisp. Remove bacon and keep it aside.
2. Place the pan back over heat. Add butter and allow it to melt. Add garlic and stir frequently for 30 – 40 seconds until fragrant.
3. Stir in the onion and cook until pink. Add leeks and Brussels sprouts and cook until tender.
4. Stir in the green onions and cook for 20 – 30 seconds. Turn off the heat and cool for a few minutes. Transfer into the bowl of mashed cauliflower.
5. Add bacon and mix well. Taste and adjust the seasoning if necessary.
6. Place a large skillet over medium heat. Add half the duck fat and swirl the pan so that the fat spreads.
7. Place 3 egg rings inside the pan. Divide equally ¼ of the parmesan cheese and sprinkle inside the rings.
8. Divide equally ¼ of the cauliflower mixture and spoon into the rings, over the parmesan.

9. Divide equally and sprinkle ¼ of the parmesan cheese over the cauliflower mixture. Cook until it is crisp at the bottom. Press slightly while it is cooking.
10. Flip sides and cook the other side until crisp.
11. Repeat steps 10-12 and make the remaining bubble n squeak.
12. Carefully remove the rings and serve.

Gluten Free Cinnamon Rolls

Number of servings: 4 – 5 cinnamon rolls

Preparation time: 30 minutes

Cooking time: 20 minutes

Ingredients:

For cinnamon rolls:

- 2 tablespoons sour cream (or coconut cream mixed with 1 teaspoon apple cider vinegar)
- ½ tablespoon inulin or maple syrup, this is required to activate the yeast
- 3.8 ounces almond flour
- 1 scoop whey protein isolate
- 1 1/8 teaspoon xanthan gum or ½ tablespoon psyllium husk powder

- ¾ teaspoon kosher salt
- 1 tablespoon grass-fed butter or ghee or coconut oil, melted, cooled
- 1 ½ tablespoons lukewarm water (around 110° F)
- ½ tablespoon active dry yeast
- 2 tablespoons golden flaxseed meal or 2 ½ tablespoons finely ground psyllium husk
- 1/8 teaspoon ground ginger
- 2 – 3 tablespoons erythritol
- 1 1/8 teaspoons baking powder
- 2 small eggs, at room temperature
- ½ tablespoon apple cider vinegar

For cinnamon filling:

- 1 ½ tablespoons unsalted grass-fed butter, softened
- 1 tablespoon ground cinnamon
- 2 – 3 tablespoons erythritol

For glaze:

- 1.6 ounces cream cheese, at room temperature

- 2 – 3 tablespoons powdered erythritol
- A pinch of kosher salt
- 1 ½ tablespoons unsalted grass-fed butter
- ½ teaspoon vanilla extract
- Heavy cream or almond milk, as required

Directions:

1. Place a sheet of parchment paper in a square-baking pan of about 9 x 9 inches.
2. Cut out a cling wrap of 12 x 12 inches square and place it on your countertop. Grease the plastic wrap with some oil. Add some water into a bowl and drop a few drops of oil into it. Place it on the countertop beside the cling wrap.

For the dough:

1. Add lukewarm water, sour cream, and maple syrup into a small bowl. Place the bowl in a double boiler. Once the temperature of the mixture is around 105° F - 110° F, remove the bowl from the double boiler. The mixture should neither be cold nor hot. This is the appropriate temperature.

2. Sprinkle yeast and ginger in a large mixing bowl. Drizzle sour cream mixture over the yeast in the bowl. Using a kitchen towel, cover the bowl. Set aside for 7 minutes.
3. The mixture should turn frothy. If it does not turn frothy, you need to redo steps 3 – 4 once again, using fresh ingredients.
4. In the meantime, combine all the dry ingredients i.e. golden flaxseed meal, almond flour, whey protein powder, xanthan gum, salt, erythritol and baking powder in a bowl. Stir until well combined.
5. When the yeast mixture is frothy, stir in the eggs, vinegar, and butter (make sure butter is cooled completely).
6. Using an electric hand mixer, mix until well incorporated. Add the mixture of dry ingredients and mix until well combined.
7. Turn the dough onto the cling wrap. Moisten your hands with the water and oil mixture and pat the dough into a rectangle.

<u>For cinnamon filling:</u>

1. Drizzle some melted butter over it and brush

it evenly. Sprinkle cinnamon and erythritol over the dough.
2. With the support of the cling wrap, tightly roll the dough into a log. Moisten your fingers and seal the edges.
3. Take a sharp knife and cut into 4 – 5 rolls. Pick up each piece and press lightly. Place it in the prepared baking dish. Leave a gap between the rolls.
4. Cover the baking dish with a kitchen towel. Place the dish in a warm area for an hour. By the end of the hour, the rolls will have risen to almost twice their original size.
5. Set the temperature of the oven to 400° F and let it preheat.
6. Place the baking sheet in the oven. Set the timer for about 17 to 25 minutes and bake the cinnamon rolls. When the cinnamon rolls are ready, they should be golden brown on top. Keep a watch over the rolls after about 17 minutes of baking.

To make glaze:

1. In the meantime, add cream cheese,

erythritol, and butter into a mixing bowl and beat with an electric hand mixer until creamy.

2. Beat in the salt and vanilla. Add heavy cream or milk, 1 teaspoon at a time and mix well each time until the consistency you desire is achieved.
3. Once baked, remove the baking sheet from the oven and drizzle glaze on top of the rolls. Let cool completely.
4. Place in an airtight container on your countertop. It can last for 2 to 3 days.
5. To heat, warm the cinnamon rolls slightly and serve.

Breakfast Quesadilla with Soft Scrambled Eggs

Number of servings: 2

Preparation time: 15 minutes

Cooking time: 10 minutes

Ingredients:

For quesadillas:

- 3 large eggs

- ½ tablespoon butter, at room temperature
- 1 chipotle pepper in adobo sauce, finely chopped
- ¼ cup shredded sharp cheddar cheese
- 2 slices bacon, cooked, crumbled
- 1 tablespoon chopped, fresh chives
- Salt to taste
- ½ can (from a 4 ounces can) diced green chilies
- 2 keto tortillas
- ¼ cup shredded Pepper Jack cheese
- A large handful baby spinach or arugula
- Extra-virgin olive oil, as required

For avocado salsa:

- ¼ cup chopped, fresh cilantro
- ½ jalapeño, deseeded, chopped
- ½ avocado, peeled, pitted, diced
- ½ tablespoon finely chopped fresh chives or green onions
- juice of ½ lime
- salt to taste

Directions:

To make avocado salsa:

1. Add avocado, salt, jalapeño, cilantro, chives and lime juice into a bowl. Stir well. Cover and set aside for a while to let the flavors blend in.
2. Add eggs and salt into a bowl and whisk well.

To make quesadilla:

1. Place a nonstick skillet over medium flame. Add butter. When butter melts, pour the beaten egg into the skillet. When the eggs are slightly set on the edges, stir the eggs and cook until soft. Turn off the heat and transfer into a bowl.
2. Add green chilies and chipotle pepper in a bowl.
3. Place a tortilla on a plate. Scatter cheese over the tortilla. Layer with eggs followed by bacon and chili mixture. Spread spinach or arugula over the chili layer.
4. Place the other tortilla over the spinach layer.

5. Place a large skillet over medium flame. Add oil and swirl the pan to spread the oil.
6. Lift the quesadilla carefully and place in the pan. When the underside is golden brown, flip sides.
7. Cook the other side until golden brown.
8. Remove the quesadilla and place on your cutting board. Cut into 4 wedges.
9. Place 2 wedges on each serving plate. Spoon some avocado salsa and serve.

Cauliflower Benedict with Dairy-free Latte

Number of servings: 2

Preparation time: 10 minutes

Cooking time: 20 minutes

Ingredients:

For cauliflower hash brown patties:

- ¼ head cauliflower, grated to rice-like texture
- ½ cup shredded cheddar cheese
- Kosher salt to taste
- 1 small egg

- ¼ teaspoon arrowroot starch
- ½ tablespoon extra-virgin olive oil

For poached eggs:

- ¼ teaspoon apple cider vinegar
- Salt to taste
- 1 large egg
- Pepper to taste

For Hollandaise sauce:

- 2 egg yolks
- ¼ cup butter
- Salt to taste
- Lemon juice to taste
- A pinch cayenne pepper or to taste

For assembling:

- 1 slice Canadian bacon
- Fresh chives, chopped, to garnish
- Paprika, to sprinkle

For dairy-free latte: Makes 1 serving

- 1 egg
- ¾ cup boiling water
- ½ teaspoon pumpkin pie spice or ground ginger
- 1 tablespoon coconut oil
- 1/8 teaspoon vanilla extract

Directions:

To make cauliflower hash brown patties:

1. Add cauliflower, cheddar cheese, salt, egg, and arrowroot into a bowl and stir until well combined.
2. Place a nonstick pan over medium-high flame. Add olive oil and swirl the pan so that the oil spreads. Let the pan heat.
3. Spoon the hash brown mixture on the heated pan and flatten it with a spoon. Instead of making 1 large hash brown, you can make 2 smaller ones. You can cook them all simultaneously.
4. Cook until the underside is golden brown. Flip sides and cook the other side until golden brown. Remove and cut into 2 halves. Keep warm.

To poach egg:

1. Place a saucepan filled with water over high heat. Bring to a boil. Add apple cider vinegar and stir.
2. Set the heat to low.
3. Crack an egg into a bowl. Stir the water to create ripples. Carefully slide the egg in the water and cook for 3 minutes. Remove the egg and place it on a serving plate. You can line it with paper towels to soak in the excess oil.

To make Hollandaise sauce:

1. Measure out the butter and melt it in a microwave or in a small pan. After poaching the egg, discard most of the water (retain about 2 inches from the bottom of the saucepan). Place a heatproof bowl over the saucepan. This will make a double boiler.
2. Pour the yolks into the heatproof bowl. Add lemon juice and mix well.
3. Pour butter in a thin drizzle, whisking simultaneously, until all of the butter is added.

4. Add salt and cayenne pepper to taste and whisk well.
5. Once the sauce is smooth and creamy, remove the bowl from the double boiler. Keeping it for longer will cook the eggs further and curds will be formed, so take it out.

To assemble:

1. Heat the bacon slice. Place cauliflower hash brown on a serving plate.
2. Place Canadian bacon on top of the hash brown. Place the poached egg over the hash brown. Spoon hollandaise sauce on top.
3. Sprinkle paprika and chives and serve with dairy-free latte.

To make dairy-free latte:

1. Add egg, water, pumpkin pie spice, coconut oil and vanilla extract into a blender and blend until frothy.
2. Pour into a cup and serve.

Breakfast Sandwiches

Number of servings: 6 – 8

Preparation time: 15 minutes

Cooking time: 45 minutes

Ingredients:

For pancake layers:

- 9 tablespoon grass-fed butter, ghee, or coconut oil, melted
- 5 large eggs
- 3 scoops Prebiotin Prebiotic Fiber
- 6 tablespoons coconut flour
- 3 scoops MCT oil powder
- 9 tablespoons heavy cream
- 1 teaspoon pure vanilla extract
- ½ teaspoon salt
- 1 teaspoon baking powder
- 1/8 teaspoon pure monk fruit extract powder

For sausage layer:

- 4 – 5 ounces sharp cheddar cheese, shredded
- 1 ½ pound pork sausage

<u>For egg layer:</u>

- 5 large eggs
- ½ teaspoon salt or to taste
- ¼ cup heavy cream
- ¼ teaspoon pepper or to taste

Directions:

1. Take 2 rimmed baking sheets (9 x 13 inches each) and place a sheet of parchment paper in each.
2. If you do not have 2 baking sheets, use one baking sheet twice to make the pancakes.

<u>To make pancake layers:</u>

1. Add melted butter, eggs, cream and vanilla into a mixing bowl. Beat with an electric hand mixer until well incorporated.
2. Add Prebiotin Prebiotic fiber, coconut flour, MCT oil powder, salt, monk fruit powder and baking powder and beat until well incorporated and free from lumps. You will have a thick batter compared to normal pancake batter.

3. Divide the batter among the prepared baking sheets. Spread it evenly.
4. Set the temperature of the oven to 400° F and let it preheat.
5. Place the baking sheets in the oven. Set the timer for about 10 minutes and bake the pancakes. When the pancakes are ready they should be golden brown on top. Cook for a few more minutes if required.
6. Cover the cooling rack with parchment paper.
7. Take out the baking sheets from the oven and upturn the baking sheets on the wire rack. Let the pancakes cool on the rack itself. Carefully remove the top parchment paper.

To make sausage layer:

1. Use one of the baking sheets and line it again with parchment paper.
2. Spread the sausage evenly on the baking sheet. Press it well.
3. Set the timer of the oven to 15 minutes and bake the sausage.
4. Once the timer goes off, scatter cheese all

over the sausage. Bake for a couple of minutes.
5. Take out the baking sheet from the oven and allow it to cool to room temperature.

To make the egg layer:

1. Use the other baking sheet and line it again with parchment paper.
2. Set the temperature of the oven to 350° F. Add eggs, salt, cream and pepper into a bowl and beat with an electric hand mixer until frothy.
3. Carefully spoon the eggs on the baking sheet. Make sure that the egg doesn't go beneath the parchment paper.
4. Place the baking sheet in the oven. Set the timer for 12 minutes or until the eggs are set.
5. Take out the baking sheet and let it cool.

To assemble:

1. Gently lift one pancake layer and place it inverted over the sausage layer. Trim off the extra sausage, if any. The extra bits of sausage can be used in some other recipe.

2. Invert the entire pancake and sausage layer on your cutting board. Now the sausage will be on top and the pancake on the bottom.
3. Carefully discard the parchment paper. Now place the egg layer over the sausage, by inverting the egg layer on the sausage layer.
4. Carefully discard the parchment paper. Place the other pancake layer, inverted, on top of the egg layer. The sandwich will have 4 layers in all.
5. Cut the large sandwich into 6 – 8 portions. Each portion will be a sandwich.
6. Serve as many as required. Wrap the remaining sandwich bars in separate parchment paper. You can store the wrapped sandwiches in an airtight container in the refrigerator or freezer.

To serve:

1. Remove from the refrigerator or freezer and thaw completely. Heat in a microwave or oven and serve.

Glazed Orange Scones with Hot Cocoa

Number of servings: 4

Preparation time: 10 minutes

Cooking time: 20 minutes

Ingredients:

For scones:

- 6 tablespoons coconut flour
- 1 teaspoon cream of tartar
- 1/8 teaspoon salt
- 1 ½ tablespoons monk fruit sweetener
- ¼ teaspoon + 1/8 teaspoon baking soda
- 2 eggs, beaten
- ½ tablespoon orange extract
- 2 tablespoons coconut oil, at room temperature
- ¼ teaspoon pure vanilla extract

For glaze:

- 3 tablespoons powdered monk fruit sweetener
- 1-2 tablespoon unsweetened
- Coconut milk, slightly warmed
- 1 tablespoon coconut oil

For garnish:

- Zest of ½ orange, grated

For hot chocolate: (Makes 1 serving)

- 1 egg
- ¾ cup boiling water
- 1 teaspoon cocoa, unsweetened
- 1 tablespoon coconut oil
- 1/8 teaspoon vanilla extract

Directions:

1. Place a sheet of parchment paper on a baking sheet.

To make scones:

1. Add all the dry ingredients (coconut flour, cream of tartar, salt, monk fruit sweetener and baking soda) into a bowl and stir until well combined.
2. Add the wet ingredients (eggs, coconut oil, orange extract, and vanilla extract) into another bowl and whisk with an electric hand mixer until well combined.

3. Add the mixture of dry ingredients into the bowl of wet ingredients and mix until well incorporated and a smooth dough is formed.
4. Turn the dough onto the prepared baking sheet. Roll the dough or pat it into a round of about 1 ½ inch thickness.
5. Slice into 4 wedges, but do not pull out the wedges. Let them remain in the round.
6. Set the temperature of the oven to 350° F and preheat the oven. Place the baking sheet in the oven. Set the timer for 18 – 20 minutes.
7. Now separate the wedges. You may need to cut them again with a knife. Let the scones cool.

To make the glaze:

1. Melt the coconut oil and add into a small blender. Add monk fruit sweetener and coconut milk and blend until well combined and a glaze is formed.
2. Add more coconut milk if the glaze is very thick and blend again.
3. Pour the glaze into a shallow bowl. Dip the

top of the scones in the glaze and place on the cooling rack. Sprinkle orange zest on top. The glaze will harden in a little while.
4. Serve scones with a cup of hot cocoa.
5. Place leftover scones in an airtight container. Place in the refrigerator. They can last for 4 – 5 days. To serve, remove from the refrigerator and bring to room temperature before serving.

To make hot cocoa:

1. Add egg, water, cocoa powder, coconut oil and vanilla extract into a blender and blend until frothy.
2. Pour into a cup and serve.

Almond Raspberry Jam Muffins

Number of servings: 6

Preparation time: 10 minutes

Cooking time: 25 minutes

Ingredients:

- 1 ½ cups almond flour
- ¾ teaspoon baking powder
- ¼ teaspoon salt
- ¼ cup granulated erythritol
- 3 tablespoons whey protein powder, unflavored
- ½ teaspoon baking soda
- ¼ cup butter, at room temperature
- 2 small eggs, at room temperature
- 10 drops stevia extract
- ½ teaspoon almond extract
- ¼ cup almond milk
- 1 tablespoon slivered almonds, to garnish

For raspberry chia jam: Makes ½ cup

- 4 ounces frozen raspberries
- 1 tablespoon water
- 1 tablespoon swerve or erythritol
- 1 tablespoon chia seeds

Directions:

To make raspberry chia jam:

1. Add raspberries, water, and erythritol into a small saucepan.

2. Place the saucepan over medium heat. Cook until soft. Stir frequently. Once the berries are soft, turn off the heat. Transfer into a bowl. Mash with a fork. Add chia seeds and stir.
3. Once it cools completely, pour into a small jar. Place in the refrigerator for about 2 hours. It will set during this time. Use as much as required and store the remaining in the refrigerator. It can last for 6 – 8 days.

<u>To make muffins:</u>

1. Line a muffin pan with disposable liners.
2. Add all the dry ingredients (almond flour, baking soda, baking powder, salt and whey protein powder) into a bowl and stir.
3. Add butter into a mixing bowl. Beat with an electric hand mixer until smooth. Beat in the erythritol. Beat for 1 – 2 minutes, until creamy and light.
4. Add eggs, one at a time and beat well each time. Scrape the sides of the bowl whenever required.
5. Add Stevia and almond extract and beat well.

6. Add half the dry ingredients mixture and almond milk and beat well. Add the rest of the dry ingredients mixture and beat until well combined.
7. Pour into the muffin cups, until each is full up to 1/3. Make a small depression in the center of each muffin. Place a teaspoon of raspberry jam in the depression.
8. Cover the depression by adding more batter into the muffin cups. Scatter almond slivers on top.
9. Set the temperature of the oven to 325° F and preheat the oven. Place the muffin pan in the oven. Set the timer for about 25 - 30 minutes or until golden brown on top.
10. Remove the muffin pan from the oven and let it cool for a few minutes.
11. Remove the muffins from the pan and cool on a wire rack.
12. Serve warm or at room temperature with vanilla milkshake. Store leftovers in an airtight container in the refrigerator. It can last for 4 to 5 days.

Vanilla Milkshake

Number of servings: 1

Preparation time: 5 minutes

Cooking time: 0 minutes

Ingredients:

- ½ teaspoon vanilla extract
- ¼ cup water
- A tiny pinch mineral salt
- ¼ cup heavy cream
- Crushed ice, as required
- Stevia to taste

Directions:

1. Add vanilla extract, cream, water, salt and Stevia into a blender and blend until smooth.
2. Pour into a glass. Fill with crushed ice and serve.

Cheddar Egg Muffins with Hot Chocolate

Number of servings: 6

Preparation time: 5 minutes

Cooking time: 8 minutes

Ingredients:

For the sausage:

- ½ tablespoon olive oil
- 1 clove garlic, minced
- ½ teaspoon dried oregano, crumbled
- ½ teaspoon dried basil
- ½ teaspoon dried parsley
- ½ teaspoon fennel seeds
- ¼ teaspoon sea salt
- 1 small yellow onion, finely chopped

- ¼ pound ground turkey
- ¼ teaspoon pepper

For muffins:

- ½ cup cheddar cheese, chopped
- ½ teaspoon dried basil
- ½ teaspoon onion powder
- ½ teaspoon dried oregano
- 1 cup finely chopped broccoli
- 2 tablespoons finely chopped, oil soaked, sun-dried tomatoes
- 4 large eggs, whisked
- ½ tablespoon chives

For hot chocolate: Makes 1 serving

- 1.5 ounces Stevia sweetened dark chocolate, chopped
- 2 tablespoons heavy cream
- 1/8 teaspoon vanilla extract
- 2 tablespoons milk of your choice
- ½ teaspoon erythritol or few drops stevia to taste

Directions:

To make sausages:

1. Place a skillet over medium heat. Add oil. When oil is heated, add onion and garlic and sauté until onion turns brown. Remove from heat and transfer into a bowl. Let it cool.
2. Add ground turkey, basil, oregano, parsley, fennel seeds and salt into the bowl of onions. Mix with your hands until well combined.
3. Shape the mixture into patties using your hands.
4. Place a nonstick skillet over medium flame and let the pan heat. Place the patties in the pan and cook until it becomes brown at the bottom. Flip sides and cook the other side until brown. It should not remain pink in the center.
5. Remove the patties and cool. When cool enough to handle, chop or crumble the patties into bite sized pieces.

To make muffins:

1. Add broccoli, sausages, cheese, tomatoes,

basil, oregano, and onion powder into a bowl. Season with salt to taste.
2. Add eggs and mix until well combined.
3. Grease 6 muffin cups with some cooking spray. Place disposable liners as well.
4. Divide the muffin mixture into the cups. Fill up to ¾ of the cup. Sprinkle chives on top.
5. Set the temperature of the oven to 350° F and preheat the oven. Place the baking sheet in the oven. Set the timer for about 25 - 30 minutes or until golden brown on top.
6. Remove the muffin pan from the oven and let it cool for a few minutes.
7. Cool slightly. Run a knife round the edges of the muffins and invert onto a plate.
8. Serve with a cup of hot chocolate.

To make hot chocolate:

1. Pour almond milk and sweetener into a small saucepan. Add sweetener and place the saucepan over medium heat. Stir frequently until sweetener dissolves completely.
2. When it begins to simmer, turn off the heat and add chocolate pieces and vanilla. Keep stirring until chocolate melts.

3. Pour into a cup and serve.

Keto Vanilla Donuts with Chocolate Glaze

Number of servings: 12

Preparation time: 10 minutes

Cooking time: 30 minutes

Ingredients:

For donuts:

- 14 teaspoons butter, melted, divided
- 2 tablespoons coconut flour
- 3 teaspoons baking powder
- ¼ teaspoon sea salt
- 4 large eggs
- 1 1/3 cups almond flour
- 6 tablespoons erythritol
- ½ teaspoon grated nutmeg
- 2 tablespoons heavy cream
- 1 teaspoon vanilla extract

For chocolate glaze:

- 2 teaspoons coconut oil
- 2 tablespoons unsweetened cocoa powder,

sifted
- 4 tablespoons unsweetened coconut flakes
- 2 ounces unsweetened baking chocolate
- 1 cup powdered erythritol
- 1 teaspoon vanilla extract
- 2 – 4 tablespoons water

Directions:

1. Grease a 12 count donut pan with 2 teaspoons melted butter.

<u>To make donuts:</u>

1. Add all the dry ingredients (almond flour, erythritol, nutmeg, coconut flour, baking powder and salt) into a bowl and stir well.
2. Add all the wet ingredients (12 teaspoons butter, eggs, cream and vanilla extract) into another bowl. Whisk well.
3. Add the wet ingredients into the bowl of dry ingredients and whisk until smooth and free from lumps.
4. Pour batter into the donut pan. Fill up to ¾.

5. Set the temperature of the oven to 350° F and preheat the oven. Place the donut pan in the oven. Set the timer for about 18 - 20 minutes or until dark golden brown on top. Rotate the pan after about 10 minutes of baking.

To make chocolate glaze:

1. Meanwhile, add chocolate and coconut oil into a heatproof bowl. Place the bowl in a double boiler. Stir frequently until the mixture melts.
2. Add cocoa powder and erythritol and whisk well.
3. Add vanilla extract and water and whisk well. The water is to be added only if the glaze is too thick.
4. While the chocolate is melting, place a pan over medium-low heat. Add coconut flakes and stir frequently until light brown. Turn off the heat and let it cool.
5. Remove the bowl from the double boiler. Dunk the top of the donuts in the glaze and place on a wire rack. Scatter toasted coconut

flakes on top of the glaze. Let it cool completely.

Crispy Sweet Cinnamon Waffles

Number of servings: 1

Preparation time: 5 minutes

Cooking time: 4 minutes

Ingredients:

For dry ingredients:

- ¼ cup super-fine almond flour
- 1/8 teaspoon baking powder
- 1/8 teaspoon baking soda
- 1/8 teaspoon salt
- 1/8 teaspoon ground cinnamon
- A pinch ground cloves
- A pinch ground nutmeg
- ¼ teaspoon erythritol

For wet ingredients:

- 1 egg, separated
- 1 tablespoon melted butter
- ½ teaspoon vanilla extract

To serve:

- Melted, salted butter
- Sugar-free maple syrup
- Any other keto friendly toppings

For sugar-free maple syrup: Makes about 1 cup

- ½ cup powdered erythritol
- ½ cup water
- ¼ teaspoon xanthan gum
- ¾ tablespoon maple extract

Directions:

To make maple syrup:

1. Add water, maple syrup and erythritol into a small saucepan.
2. Place the saucepan over medium heat. When it begins to boil, lower the heat and simmer for a few minutes until erythritol has dissolved.
3. Turn off the heat and pour into a blender. Sprinkle xanthan gum on top and blend until smooth. Let it cool.
4. Pour into a squeeze bottle. Refrigerate until

use. It can be used with waffles, donuts, pancakes, etc.

To make waffles:

1. Add all the dry ingredients (almond flour, baking powder, baking soda, salt, cinnamon, cloves, nutmeg and erythritol) into a bowl and stir well.
2. Beat the egg white with an electric hand mixer until stiff peaks are formed.
3. Add egg yolk, butter and vanilla into a bowl and whisk well. Pour into the bowl of dry ingredients and stir.
4. Add egg white and fold gently until the batter is smooth.
5. Plug in your waffle maker and let it preheat. Grease the waffle maker and pour the batter into the waffle maker. Close the lid and cook until crisp, 4 – 6 minutes.
6. Remove the waffle from the waffle maker and drizzle melted butter over it.
7. Serve with sugar-free maple syrup.

Keto Fluffy Pancakes with Nutella (Chocolate Hazelnut Spread)

Number of servings: 2

Preparation time: 10 minutes

Cooking time: 45 minutes

Ingredients:

For pancakes:

- 2 tablespoons coconut flour
- ½ cup almond flour
- ½ teaspoon salt
- ¼ teaspoon ground cinnamon (optional)
- 1 tablespoon erythritol or xylitol
- ½ teaspoon baking powder
- 3 eggs, at room temperature
- 1 tablespoon butter, melted
- 2 tablespoons heavy whipping cream, at room temperature
- ½ teaspoon vanilla extract
- Butter, as required to make pancakes

For Nutella: Makes 1 cup

- ½ cup peeled hazelnuts
- ¼ cup almonds
- ½ cup macadamia nuts

- 1.75 ounces keto friendly dark chocolate
- 1 tablespoon powdered erythritol or swerve
- ¼ teaspoon vanilla powder or ½ teaspoon pure vanilla extract
- ¼ cup warm coconut milk or heavy whipping cream (optional)
- ½ tablespoon virgin coconut oil
- ½ tablespoon cacao powder
- Stevia drops to taste (optional)

Directions:

To make Nutella:

1. Take a baking sheet and place macadamia nuts, hazelnuts, and almonds on it. Spread it evenly, in a single layer.
2. Set the temperature of the oven to 375° F and preheat the oven. Place the baking sheet in the oven. Set the timer for about 8 - 10 minutes or until light brown.
3. Remove the baking sheet from the oven and let the nuts cool.
4. Add chocolate and coconut oil into a heatproof bowl and place it in a double boiler. Stir frequently until the mixture

melts. Remove the bowl from the double boiler.

5. Add nuts into the food processor bowl and process until smooth. Add chocolate mixture, vanilla, cacao powder and erythritol and blend until smooth.
6. Spoon into a jar. Use as much as required. Place in the refrigerator. It can last for 3 months.
7. If you are adding heavy cream or coconut milk, add it in step 5. It can last only for a week in the refrigerator.

To make pancakes:

1. Add all the dry ingredients (coconut flour, almond flour, baking powder, salt and cinnamon) into a bowl and stir until well combined.
2. Add eggs, butter, cream and vanilla and whisk until the batter is just combined. Do not over-beat.
3. Place a griddle pan over medium-high heat. Grease it with some butter or oil.
4. Pour half the batter on the griddle. In a

minute or so, slowly bubbles will be visible. Cook until it becomes brown at the bottom. Flip sides and cook the other side.
5. Remove the pancake and keep warm in an oven.
6. Repeat the previous step and make the other pancake.
7. Serve pancakes with Nutella or sugar-free maple syrup.

To make Nutella sandwich pancakes:

1. Once you are done with step 5, place a sheet of parchment paper on a baking sheet. Place about 2 tablespoons of Nutella on the baking sheet. Spread it with the back of a spoon into a round shape. Repeat this for as many sandwiches as you require.
2. Freeze for 20 – 30 minutes until firm. Have your pancake batter ready (steps 8 – 9).
3. Place a griddle pan over medium-high heat. Grease it with some butter or oil.
4. Pour ¼ of the batter on the griddle. Place a frozen Nutella round on it. Spread ¼ of the batter over the frozen Nutella round.

5. In a minute or so, bubbles will be visible. Cook until it becomes brown at the bottom. Flip sides and cook the other side.
6. Remove pancakes and serve.
7. Repeat steps 17 – 20 and make the other sandwich pancake. Top with strawberry slices and serve.

Overnight Chia Pudding

Number of servings: 10

Preparation time: 10 hours

Cooking time: 0 mins

For chia pudding:

- ¾ cup chia seeds
- 3 cups full fat coconut milk
- 3 cups unsweetened almond milk
- Stevia drops to taste
- 1 teaspoon ground cinnamon
- 1 teaspoons pure vanilla extract
- 1/8 teaspoon salt

To make chia pudding:

1. Add almond milk, coconut milk, stevia drops, ground cinnamon, salt and vanilla extract into a bowl and stir until well combined. Taste and add more stevia drops if required.
2. Add 1-tablespoon chia seeds at a time and stir well each time. When all the chia seeds are added, give one last stir. Cover the bowl and place in the refrigerator all night.
3. With the ingredients given in this pudding recipe, ten servings will be made. You can store the extra chia pudding in an airtight container in the refrigerator. Leftover chia

KETOGENIC LUNCH RECIPES

Keto Chicken Salad with Avocado

Number of servings: 1

Preparation time: 10 minutes

Cooking time: 20 – 30 minutes

Ingredients:

For chicken:

- 1 boneless chicken thigh fillet
- 1 tablespoon olive oil
- ¼ teaspoon pepper
- ½ teaspoon dried thyme
- 2 tablespoons water
- ½ teaspoon salt

- ½ teaspoon sweet chili powder
- 2 cloves garlic, peeled, lightly crushed

For salad:

- 1 cup arugula
- A handful fresh basil leaves, torn
- ½ cup halved cherry tomatoes
- ½ cup Purslane leaves
- ¼ cup chopped fresh dill
- ½ tablespoon sliced olives
- ½ teaspoon sesame seeds
- 1 teaspoon olive oil
- ½ avocado sliced
- ½ teaspoon nigella seeds
- Ranch dressing to taste

For ranch dressing:

- ¼ cup sour cream
- 2 tablespoons heavy whipping cream
- ½ teaspoon dried dill
- ½ teaspoon garlic powder
- Pepper to taste
- ½ teaspoon onion powder
- Salt to taste

- ½ teaspoon chopped chives
- ¼ cup keto friendly mayonnaise
- Lemon juice to taste

Directions:

To make ranch dressing:

1. Add sour cream, heavy whipping cream dried dill, garlic powder, pepper, onion powder, salt, chives, mayonnaise and lemon juice into a bowl and stir. Use as much as required.
2. Store the remaining in a small jar. Refrigerate until use. It can last for 4 – 5 days. You can use it as a dip or in some other recipe.

To make chicken:

1. Place a skillet over medium-low heat. Add chicken and water and cover with a lid. Cook until chicken is cooked through. Turn the chicken around every 4 – 5 minutes.
2. Remove the lid. Pour oil over the chicken. Add garlic, pepper, salt, thyme and chili powder. Stir well.

3. Cover and cook until chicken is golden brown. Turn the chicken around every 4 – 5 minutes. Turn off the heat.
4. Remove the chicken from the pan and place it on your cutting board. When cool enough to handle, cut it into slices.

To assemble the salad:

1. Scatter arugula, basil, Purslane and dill on a serving platter. Scatter olives and avocado slices. Place chicken slices on top. Sprinkle nigella and sesame seeds on top.
2. Drizzle as much dressing as required and serve. You can also use creamy avocado dressing, the recipe of which is given in the next recipe – Garlic butter tilapia salad with creamy avocado dressing.

Garlic Butter Tilapia Salad with Creamy Avocado Dressing

Number of servings: 3

Preparation time: 10 minutes

Cooking time: 8 – 10 minutes

Ingredients:

<u>For salad:</u>

- 7 ounces tilapia fillets, well rinsed
- 1.5 ounces cherry tomatoes, halved
- ½ medium yellow bell pepper, cut into strips
- 1 ½ tablespoons butter
- ¼ teaspoon onion powder
- 1-2 tablespoons fresh lemon juice or to taste
- 3.5 ounces spinach
- ½ avocado, peeled, pitted, sliced
- ½ small cucumber, thinly sliced
- 3 cloves garlic, finely chopped
- ¼ teaspoon Spanish paprika
- Salt to taste
- Freshly ground pepper to taste

<u>Creamy avocado dressing:</u>

- ½ avocado, peeled, pitted, chopped
- A large pinch ground sage
- A large pinch dried basil
- 3 tablespoons yogurt
- Stevia drops or erythritol to taste
- 1 tablespoon fresh lemon juice

Directions:

To make salad:

1. Dry the tilapia fillets by patting with paper towels. Sprinkle salt, pepper, paprika and onion powder on the fillets.
2. Grease a baking dish with some cooking spray and line it with foil. Place the tilapia fillets, bell pepper and tomatoes in the baking dish.
3. Brush butter over the fillets. Scatter garlic all over.
4. Set the temperature of the oven to 400° F and preheat the oven. Place the baking dish in the oven. Set the timer for about for 12-14 minutes or until the fillets flake easily when pierced with a fork.
5. Remove the baking dish from the oven and let it cool for a few minutes.

To make dressing:

1. Add avocado, yogurt, sage, basil and lemon juice into a blender. Blend until smooth.

To assemble the salad:

1. Spread spinach on a serving platter. Place fillets over it in a single layer.
2. Scatter avocado, bell pepper, cucumber and tomatoes. Sprinkle lemon juice on top.
3. Spoon the dressing on top and serve.

Chicken Zoodle Soup

Number of servings: 3

Preparation time: 10 minutes

Cooking time: 12 – 15 minutes

Ingredients:

For chicken noodle soup:

- 1 tablespoon olive oil

- 1 ½ stalks celery, diced
- 2 small cloves garlic, minced
- 1 cup cooked, shredded chicken
- ¼ teaspoon dried basil
- ¼ teaspoon dried oregano
- ½ teaspoon salt or to taste
- 2 large zucchinis, trimmed
- 1 small onion, diced
- ½ red bell pepper, diced
- 3 cups chicken stock
- ½ teaspoon pepper

To serve:

- Mozzarella cheese balls

Directions:

1. Place a soup pot over medium heat. Add oil and allow it to warm.
2. Once oil is heated, add onion and sauté for a couple of minutes.
3. Add garlic and cook for a few seconds until aromatic.
4. Add celery and pepper and stir fry for a few minutes until the vegetables are tender.

5. Pour chicken stock into the pot and stir.
6. Stir in oregano, basil, chicken, pepper and salt. Bring to a boil.
7. Lower the heat and simmer.
8. Meanwhile, make noodles of the zucchini using a spiralizer or julienne peeler.
9. Add the zucchini noodles into the pot and simmer until the zucchini noodles are cooked to the desired doneness.
10. Taste and adjust the seasonings if required. Turn off the heat.
11. Ladle into soup bowls.
12. Scatter some mozzarella cheese on top and serve.

Spicy Chicken Nuggets

Number of servings: 2

Preparation time: 15 minutes

Cooking time: 15 – 20 minutes

Ingredients:

For marinade:

- 8.8 ounces boneless chicken breast or thighs, chop into bite sized pieces, rinsed well

- ½ tablespoon white wine vinegar
- 1 clove garlic, pressed
- Salt to taste
- ¼ cup sour cream or full-fat coconut milk
- ½ teaspoon poultry seasoning
- Freshly ground pepper to taste
- ¼ teaspoon chili powder
- Cayenne pepper to taste

For breading:

- 4 – 8 tablespoons almond flour
- 1.5 ounces pork rinds
- ½ teaspoon dried oregano
- ¼ teaspoon garlic powder
- Freshly ground pepper to taste
- ½ teaspoon onion powder
- Cayenne pepper to taste
- 1 small egg, beaten
- 2 tablespoons finely grated parmesan cheese
- ¼ teaspoon paprika

For cheese dip:

- 3 tablespoons heavy whipping cream
- 1/3 cup shredded sharp cheddar cheese

- 1 ounce cream cheese
- 1/8 teaspoon salt or to taste

Directions:

1. Dry the chicken by patting with paper towels.

To make marinade:

1. Add sour cream, poultry seasoning, garlic, vinegar, salt, pepper, chili powder and cayenne pepper into a bowl and stir until well combined.
2. Add chicken into the bowl and stir until the chicken is well coated with the marinade.
3. Cover the bowl with plastic wrap. Refrigerate for 2 – 8 hours, the longer the better.
4. Place a sheet of parchment paper on a baking sheet.
5. Remove the bowl from the refrigerator.
6. Set the temperature of the oven to 425° F and preheat the oven.

For breading:

1. Place almond flour in a shallow bowl.
2. Place pork rinds, salt, pepper, oregano, parmesan cheese, cayenne pepper, onion and garlic powder in another bowl.
3. Add egg and sour cream into a 3rd bowl and whisk well.
4. Pick out the chicken nuggets from the marinade, a few pieces at a time, and dredge in almond flour. Shaking off excess flour, dip in the egg mixture.
5. Shaking off excess egg, dredge in the pork rind mixture and place on the prepared baking sheet.
6. Place the baking sheet in the oven. Set the timer for about 15 – 20 minutes or until nuggets are golden brown and crisp.

To make cheese dip:

1. While the nuggets are baking, add whipping cream and cream cheese into a small pot.
2. Place the pot over medium-low heat. Stir frequently until the mixture melts.
3. Turn off the heat. Stir in cheddar cheese and salt. Mix until cheddar cheese melts.
4. Serve chicken nuggets with cheese dip.

Keto Lunch Bento Box

Number of servings: 12 muffins

Preparation time: 10 minutes

Cooking time: 20 minutes

Ingredients:

For muffins:

- 4 cups chopped, fresh spinach
- 6 tablespoons half and half
- Salt to taste
- ½ cup shredded mozzarella cheese
- Pepper to taste
- 6 eggs
- ¼ cup water

To serve:

- Cheddar cheese or Monterey Jack cheese
- Cucumber slices
- Turkey or ham slices, cooked
- Fresh berries of your choice

Directions:

To make muffins:

1. Add spinach into a microwave safe bowl. Sprinkle water over it.
2. Cover the dish with plastic wrap (that is microwave safe). Make a hole at one side for the steam to escape. Cook on high for 40 – 50 seconds or until spinach wilts.
3. Remove the bowl from the microwave and discard the liquid from the bowl. Squeeze the spinach of excess moisture.
4. Crack the eggs into a bowl. Whisk well. Add salt and pepper to taste and whisk well.
5. Add spinach and mozzarella cheese and whisk.
6. Grease a 12 count muffin pan with some cooking spray. Place disposable liners in each cup.
7. Divide equally the egg mixture and pour it into the muffin cups.
8. Set the temperature of the oven to 425° F and preheat the oven.
9. Place the muffin pan in the oven. Set the timer for about 25 - 30 minutes or until golden brown on top.

10. Remove the muffin pan from the oven and let it cool for a few minutes.
11. Remove the muffins from the pan and cool on a wire rack.

To serve:

1. Place 1 – 2 muffins in the lunch box. Place cheese slices, cooked ham slices or turkey slices and some berries along with the muffins and serve.

Pizza with Topping Options

Number of servings: 4

Preparation time: 15 minutes

Cooking time: 15 – 20 minutes

Ingredients:

For pizza crust:

- 6 tablespoons super fine almond flour
- 1 tablespoon cream cheese, softened
- 1 cup finely shredded mozzarella cheese
- A pinch salt
- ½ teaspoon garlic powder

For pizza sauce:

- ¼ onion, chopped
- 2 tablespoons olive oil
- 1 ½ cups canned crushed tomatoes or diced tomatoes
- 1 teaspoon dried parsley
- 1 teaspoon dried oregano
- 1 teaspoon Lakanto golden sweetener
- Salt to taste
- ½ teaspoon chili flakes
- Pepper to taste
- 2 cloves garlic, peeled, minced
- 3 tablespoons tomato paste

For toppings: Use any one or more

- Shredded cheese of your choice like mozzarella, parmesan, feta cheese, etc.
- Cooked meat of your choice
- Any other keto sauce to top instead of the regular pizza sauce like ranch dressing, buffalo sauce, blue cheese dressing, pesto, etc.
- Red pepper flakes
- Dried herbs of your choice

- Chopped vegetables of your choice like onion, bell pepper, sliced olives, jalapeños, etc.

Directions:

To make pizza crust:

1. Shift the rack to the middle of the oven. Set the temperature of the oven to 425° F and preheat the oven.
2. Add almond flour, cream cheese, mozzarella cheese, garlic powder and salt into a saucepan.
3. Place the saucepan over low heat. Stir continuously until the mixture melts and is like dough. Turn off the heat.
4. Place a sheet of parchment paper on your countertop. Remove the dough from the saucepan. Form into a thick round and place on the parchment paper.
5. Place another sheet of parchment paper on top of the dough.
6. Roll with a rolling pin until about 6 – 7 inches in diameter or the thickness of the crust you desire is achieved.
7. Peel off the top parchment paper. Lift the

pizza crust along with the parchment paper and place on a baking sheet.
8. Pierce the dough all over using a fork.
9. Place the baking sheet in the oven.
10. Set the timer for 6 – 8 minutes and bake the crust until light golden brown.
11. Remove the baking sheet from the oven and flip the crust.
12. Reduce the temperature of the oven to 350° F
13. Place the baking sheet in the oven and bake for 3 – 5 minutes.

To make pizza sauce:

1. While the crust is baking, place a skillet over medium flame.
2. Add oil and let it heat. Add onion and cook for a couple of minutes. Add garlic and cook for a few seconds until fragrant.
3. Stir in the tomato paste and cook for a minute. Next, add the tomatoes along with parsley, oregano, red chili flakes, salt, pepper and sweetener and mix well.
4. Lower the heat and simmer until the sauce is thick. Stir occasionally.

To top the pizza:

1. Spread pizza sauce on top or use any other sauce of your choice.
2. Place any of the suggested toppings on the crust.
3. Place the pizza in the oven and bake for a few minutes until the cheese melts.
4. Cut into 4 wedges and serve.

Ham and Cheese Sandwich Braid

Number of servings: 12

Preparation time: 30 minutes

Cooking time: 24 minutes

Ingredients:

For sauce:

- 4 tablespoons keto friendly mayonnaise
- 4 teaspoons mustard
- 2 teaspoons minced, fresh thyme leaves

For the dough:

- 3 cups super fine almond flour

- ½ teaspoon salt
- 2 large eggs
- 4 cups mozzarella cheese, cut into chunks
- 2 teaspoons xanthan gum
- 4 teaspoons baking powder
- 2 ounces cream cheese, at room temperature

For assembling:

- 8 ounces thinly sliced ham
- 2 medium eggs, whisked (optional)
- 6 slices provolone cheese, halved
- 2 teaspoons sesame seeds (optional)

Directions:

1. To make sauce: Add mayonnaise, mustard and thyme leaves into a bowl and stir. Cover and set aside for a while for the flavors to blend in.
2. To make dough: Place almond flour, salt, xanthan gum and baking powder in the food processor bowl. Process until well combined.
3. Crack the eggs into the food processor. Add cream cheese and mozzarella cheese.

Blend until well combined and resembles dough.

4. Remove the mixture from the food processor and place in a heavy bottomed saucepan.
5. Place the saucepan over low heat. Stir continuously until the cheese melts and is gooey. Turn off the heat.
6. Remove half the dough from the saucepan.
7. Place a sheet of parchment paper on your countertop. Form the dough into a ball and place on the parchment paper.
8. Place another sheet of parchment paper on top of the dough.
9. Roll with a rolling pin until it is a rectangle of 10 x 15 inches.
10. Peel off the top parchment paper. Lift the pizza crust along with the parchment paper and place on a large baking sheet. If your baking sheet is not large enough, use 2 baking sheets and bake in batches.

To assemble:

1. Divide the rectangle into 3 equal portions, along the length (that means each portion is

about 3 ½ inches). Using a sharp knife, cut strips of 1 ½ inches width, in a slant position on either side of the central portion. This is to make braids. There should be same number of strips on either side.

2. Smear half the sauce on the central portion. Place half the ham slices over the sauce layer. Next layer with half the provolone cheese.
3. Fold the strips over the filling, one from either side, starting from one end. So, it will look braided. The last strip should be tucked below.
4. Beat egg in a bowl and brush the top of the dough strips with egg. Scatter sesame seeds on top.
5. Pick up the parchment paper along with the dough and place on a baking sheet.
6. Repeat steps 6 – 15 and make the other sandwich braid.
7. Set the temperature of the oven to 375° F and preheat the oven.
8. Place the baking sheet in the oven and set the temperature for 23 – 28 minutes or until slightly golden brown on top.
9. Remove the sandwich braid from the oven. Cut each into 6 slices and serve.

10. You can store one of the loaves in an airtight container in the refrigerator. It can last for 4 – 5 days.

Keto Peanut Butter and Jelly Sandwiches

Number of servings: 1

Preparation time: 2 minutes

Cooking time: 1-½ minutes

Ingredients:

- 1 large egg
- ½ tablespoon coconut flour
- 1 ½ tablespoons almond flour
- ¼ teaspoon baking powder

- ½ tablespoon butter

For jelly: Makes about ½ cup

- ¼ + 1/8 teaspoon gelatin powder
- 4 ounces frozen raspberries
- 2 tablespoons water
- 1 teaspoon lemon juice
- ¼ teaspoon monk fruit sweetener

To serve:

- Jelly
- Peanut butter

Directions:

To make jelly:

1. Place lemon juice in a bowl. Scatter gelatin over it.
2. Add raspberries, water, and monk fruit sweetener into a saucepan. Place the saucepan over medium flame.
3. When it begins to bubble, lower the heat and simmer for about 10 – 12 minutes. Turn off the heat.

4. Add gelatin mixture into the saucepan and mix until it dissolves completely. Transfer into a bowl. Once it cools, cover with plastic wrap and chill until use. It can last for a week.

To make bread:

1. Add coconut flour, almond flour, baking powder, egg and butter into a microwave safe mug and stir until well combined.
2. Place the mug in the microwave and cook on high for 90 seconds.
3. Remove the bread from the microwave and let it cool.
4. Cut into 2 slices.

To make sandwich:

1. Spread peanut butter on one slice of bread and jelly on the other and close the sandwich.

Fish Fingers / Sticks with Chimichurri Mayo

Number of servings: 1

Preparation time: 10 minutes

Cooking time: 13 – 15 minutes

Ingredients:

- 4.4 ounces white fish like cod, cut into 1 inch thick slices, like fingers
- 3 tablespoons almond flour
- ¼ teaspoon onion powder
- 1/8 teaspoon paprika
- 1/8 teaspoon garlic powder
- ¼ teaspoon salt or to taste
- 1 small egg, lightly beaten

For chimichurri sauce:

- A handful fresh parsley, finely chopped
- 2 cloves garlic, chopped
- 1 tablespoon apple cider vinegar or freshly squeezed lime juice
- ¼ teaspoon salt
- 2 tablespoons finely chopped fresh oregano
- ½ small red chili pepper, deseeded
- ¼ cup extra-virgin olive oil
- 1/8 teaspoon pepper or to taste
- 2 tablespoons keto friendly mayonnaise

To serve:

- Lemon wedges
- Dressed greens (optional)

Directions:

1. Set the temperature of the oven to 375° F and preheat the oven.
2. Place a sheet of parchment paper or foil on a baking sheet. Spray some cooking spray over it.

To make fish fingers:

1. Crack egg into a bowl and beat well.
2. Add almond flour, garlic powder, onion powder, salt, pepper, and paprika into a shallow bowl and stir until well combined.
3. Dip the fish fingers in the egg, one at a time. Shaking off excess egg, dredge the fish fingers in almond flour mixture. Shaking off excess almond flour mixture, place the fish fingers on the prepared baking sheet.
4. Place the baking sheet in the oven and set the timer for 13 minutes. Flip sides after 7 –

8 minutes of baking. Bake until golden brown.

To make chimichurri mayonnaise:

1. Place mayonnaise in a bowl.
2. Add parsley, garlic, vinegar, salt, oregano, red chili pepper, extra-virgin olive oil, and pepper into a blender.
3. Blend until the sauce is smooth in texture.
4. Pour into the bowl of mayonnaise. Taste and add more seasoning and vinegar if required.

Keto Grilled Cheese with Tomato Soup

Number of servings: 2

Preparation time: 3 minutes

Cooking time: 8 – 10 minutes

Ingredients:

For tomato soup:

- 2 teaspoons olive oil or butter
- 1 clove garlic, peeled, sliced
- Pepper to taste
- ½ teaspoon dried basil

- ¼ teaspoon dried oregano
- ¼ teaspoon salt or to taste
- 6 ounces canned, peeled tomatoes
- 2 teaspoons tomato paste
- 2 tablespoons chopped onion
- 1 – 1 ½ cups water
- 4 tablespoons crumbled feta cheese
- 2 tablespoons heavy cream or almond milk

For bread:

- 6 tablespoons almond flour
- ½ teaspoon baking powder
- Salt to taste
- 2 eggs
- 1 tablespoon butter
- 2 tablespoons grated cheddar cheese
- 2 tablespoons parmesan cheese
- ½ teaspoon onion powder
- 2 tablespoons olive oil

For filling:

- 2 tablespoons mayonnaise
- 2 slices cheddar cheese

Directions:

To make tomato soup:

1. Place a soup pot over medium heat. Add butter. When butter melts, add onion and sauté until translucent.
2. Stir in the garlic and cook for about a minute.
3. Stir in the tomato paste, tomatoes, salt, pepper, oregano and basil.
4. Add water and mix well. Bring to a simmer.
5. Lower the heat and cook for about 10 minutes or until tomatoes are soft. Turn off the heat. Blend with an immersion blender until smooth.

To make bread:

1. Add almond flour, baking powder, salt, parmesan cheese, and onion powder into a square shaped microwave safe dish. Stir until well combined.
2. Add eggs and olive oil and mix until well incorporated and free from lumps.
3. Place in the microwave. Cook on high for 110 seconds. If the bread looks uncooked

after 110 seconds, cook for 10 – 20 seconds until well cooked.

4. Remove the dish from the microwave. Invert the container on a plate. Once it cools, cut the bread into 4 slices, horizontally.

<u>To make grilled cheese sandwiches:</u>

1. Place a skillet over medium-high heat. Add half the butter and swirl the pan to spread the butter.
2. Fry 2 slices of bread until light golden on one side. Turn the bread slices.
3. Spread mayonnaise on the top of each piece of bread. Place a cheese slice on one slice of bread. Cover the sandwich with the other slice of bread, with the mayonnaise side touching the cheese.
4. When the underside is golden brown, flip the entire sandwich and cook the other side until golden brown.
5. Repeat steps 5 – 8 and make the other sandwich.
6. Heat up the soup just before serving, adding feta cheese and almond milk.
7. Serve grilled sandwich with tomato soup.

Keto Sandwich Bowl

Number of servings: 2

Preparation time: 10 minutes

Cooking time: 0 minutes

Ingredients:

For sandwich bowl:

- 10 slices smoked deli ham, chopped
- 6 slices provolone cheese, chopped
- 8 banana peppers, chopped
- 2/3 orange bell pepper, chopped
- 2 cups chopped romaine hearts
- 6 pickles, chopped
- 1 cucumber, chopped
- 6 cherry tomatoes, halved

For dressing:

- 4 tablespoons olive oil
- ½ teaspoon Italian seasoning
- 8 teaspoons red wine vinegar
- Salt to taste
- Pepper to taste

Directions:

To make dressing:

1. Whisk together olive oil, Italian seasoning, salt, pepper and red wine vinegar. Set aside for a few minutes for the flavors to blend in.

To make a sandwich bowl:

1. Divide the ham, cheese, banana peppers, orange bell pepper, romaine hearts, pickles, cucumber and cherry tomatoes into 2 bowls.
2. Drizzle the dressing among the bowls.
3. Toss well. Cover and set aside for at least 30 minutes for the flavors to blend in.
4. Toss once again before serving.

Tuna-Stuffed Tomatoes

Number of servings: 2

Preparation time: 15 minutes

Cooking time: 0 minutes

Ingredients:

- 1 can (3 ounce) oil packed tuna, drained

- 4 small tomatoes
- ¼ teaspoons fresh thyme leaves, minced
- 5 kalamata olives, pitted, minced
- ½ tablespoons capers, drained, rinsed
- 1 tablespoons fresh parsley, minced
- 1 tablespoons olive oil
- Salt to taste
- Pepper to taste

Directions:

1. Slice off the tops of each tomato thinly and scoop the seeds and pulp, discarding each.
2. Place the tomato shells on paper towels with cut sides on the paper towels.
3. Mix the rest of the ingredients in a bowl and mash the tuna into smaller pieces. Fill the tomatoes with the mixture.
4. Serve.

Garlic Butter Chicken with Broccoli Salad

Number of servings: 2

Preparation time: 15 minutes

Cooking time: 20 minutes

Ingredients:

For garlic butter chicken:

- 1 medium chicken breast
- ½ teaspoon Italian seasoning
- Crushed red chili flakes to taste
- 2 cloves garlic, minced
- ½ tablespoon olive oil
- Salt to taste
- 1 tablespoon butter
- Pepper to taste
- 1 tablespoon finely chopped, fresh parsley or cilantro

For broccoli salad:

- 1 medium head broccoli, cut into bite size florets
- 2 tablespoons thinly sliced red onion
- 1 ½ slices bacon, cooked, crumbled
- Salt to taste
- ¼ cup shredded cheddar cheese
- 2 tablespoons toasted, sliced almonds
- 1 tablespoon chopped fresh chives

For dressing:

- 1/3 cup keto friendly mayonnaise
- ½ tablespoon Dijon mustard
- Freshly ground pepper to taste
- 1 ½ tablespoons apple cider vinegar
- Salt to taste

Directions:

To make dressing:

1. Add mayonnaise, Dijon mustard, pepper, apple cider vinegar, and salt into a bowl and stir well. Cover and set aside for a while for the flavors to blend in.

To make broccoli salad:

1. Place a saucepan half filled with water over medium heat. Add a little salt and bring to a boil.
2. Drop the broccoli florets into the boiling water. Cook for a couple of minutes until they turn bright green in color.
3. Drain off the water and immerse the broccoli in a bowl of ice water.
4. Once the broccoli cools down, drain off the water and set aside in a bowl.
5. Pour the dressing over the broccoli and stir until well coated. Cover and refrigerate until use.

To make garlic butter chicken:

1. First cut the chicken breast into 2 halves horizontally and then sprinkle salt, pepper, Italian seasoning and crushed red pepper over the chicken.
2. Place a pan over medium-high heat. Add oil and let it heat. Swirl the pan so that the oil spreads.
3. Place the chicken in the pan and cook until the underside is golden brown. Flip sides

and cook the other side until golden brown. Remove chicken and place on a plate.
4. Lower the heat to medium-low. Add butter. When butter melts, add garlic, crushed red pepper flakes and parsley and stir for 15 – 20 seconds.
5. Add the chicken back into the pan. Spoon the butter sauce over the chicken. Cook until garlic turns golden brown.
6. Divide into 2 plates. Serve chicken with butter sauce along with broccoli salad.

Easy Meatball Subs

Number of servings: 3

Preparation time: 15 minutes

Cooking time: 30 minutes

Ingredients:

- 2 teaspoons olive oil
- 1 teaspoon dried oregano
- ½ can (from a 28 ounces can) crushed tomatoes
- ¼ teaspoon erythritol

- 3 keto hot dog buns (recipe to make buns is given in the next chapter, in the 1st recipe)
- 1 clove garlic, peeled, pressed
- Red pepper flakes to taste
- ¼ teaspoon salt or to taste
- Italian meatballs, for filling in the sandwich
- Shredded mozzarella cheese or fresh mozzarella cheese balls as required

For Italian meatballs:

- ½ pound ground beef
- 1 small egg
- ¼ teaspoon dried basil
- ½ teaspoon garlic powder
- ¼ teaspoon onion powder
- ¼ teaspoon pepper or to taste
- 1 ounce parmesan cheese, grated
- ½ teaspoon salt or to taste
- 1 ½ tablespoons olive oil

Directions:

To make meatballs:

1. Add beef, egg, basil, garlic powder, onion

powder, pepper, parmesan cheese and salt into a bowl and stir well.
2. Make small meatballs of the mixture. You can moisten your hand with some water while shaping into meatballs.
3. Place a skillet over medium flame. Add oil. Swirl the pan so that the oil spreads.
4. Once oil is heated, add meatballs and cook until golden brown all over. Remove the meatballs and set aside on a plate.

To make sauce:

1. Place the same pan back over medium heat. Add oil and let it heat.
2. Add garlic, red pepper flakes, and oregano and stir continuously for a few seconds until aromatic, taking care not to burn the oregano and red pepper flakes.
3. Reduce the heat to low heat. Stir in the tomatoes, erythritol and salt and cook for 10 – 12 minutes.
4. Add the meatballs back into the pan. Mix until the meatballs are well coated in the sauce. Cover and cook for about 15 – 20

minutes. Stir every 7 – 8 minutes. Turn off the heat.

5. Make slit in the buns, along the length of the bun. Fill the slit with sauce-covered meatballs. Place the buns on a baking sheet. Place cheese on top.
6. Place the rack in the topmost position. Set the oven to broil mode and preheat the oven.
7. Place the baking sheet in the oven. Broil for a couple of minutes until the cheese melts.

7

KETOGENIC DINNER RECIPES

Hot Dogs

Number of servings: 3

Preparation time: 15 minutes

Cooking time: 25 minutes

Ingredients:

For hot dog buns:

- 1 egg, at room temperature
- 1 egg white, at room temperature
- 1 cup almond flour
- 2 tablespoons psyllium husk or psyllium husk powder
- ¼ teaspoon xanthan gum

- ¼ cup warm water
- 2 tablespoons butter, melted
- ¾ teaspoon baking powder
- A pinch salt

For hot dog filling:

- 3 medium gluten-free sausages
- 2 tablespoons shredded white cabbage
- 2 tablespoons shredded red cabbage
- 1 ½ teaspoons extra-virgin olive oil
- ½ tablespoon sugar-free tomato ketchup
- 1 ½ tablespoons chopped parsley
- 1 teaspoon Dijon mustard

Directions:

To make hot dog buns:

1. Add egg and egg white into a bowl and whisk well.
2. Add almond flour, psyllium husk, xanthan gum, warm water, butter, baking powder and salt and mix with your hands until you have smooth dough, taking care not to over-mix.
3. Line a baking sheet with parchment paper.

4. Divide the dough into 3 equal portions, give each portion the shape of a small log, and place on the baking sheet. Leave sufficient gap between the breads.
5. Set the temperature of the oven to 375° F and preheat the oven.
6. Place the baking sheet in the oven. Set the timer for 35 minutes or until golden brown on top.
7. Take out the baked hot dog buns and set aside to cool.
8. Meanwhile, cook the sausages following the directions on the package.

To make slaw:

1. Add green cabbage, red cabbage and parsley into a bowl and toss well.
2. Drizzle olive oil and toss well.
3. Make a slit in the center of the hot dog bun, along the length of the bun. Fill each with a sausage and slaw. Dot with Dijon mustard and ketchup and serve.

Keto Meatballs with Spaghetti

Number of servings: 2

Preparation time: 15 minutes

Cooking time: 30 minutes

Ingredients:

For meatballs:

- ½ pound ground beef
- ¼ cup shredded mozzarella cheese
- 1 tablespoon chopped fresh parsley
- ½ teaspoon kosher salt or to taste
- 1 tablespoon extra-virgin olive oil
- 2 small cloves garlic, peeled, minced
- 2 tablespoons freshly grated parmesan cheese + extra to serve

- 1 small egg, beaten
- ¼ teaspoon freshly ground pepper or to taste

For sauce:

- ½ medium onion, chopped
- ½ can (from a 28 ounces can) crushed tomatoes
- Kosher salt to taste
- 1 clove garlic, peeled, minced
- ½ teaspoon dried oregano
- Freshly ground pepper to taste

For zucchini noodles (spaghetti):

- 1 medium zucchini, trimmed
- ½ tablespoon olive oil
- 1 tablespoon grated parmesan cheese
- Salt to taste
- 1 clove garlic, peeled, minced
- Pepper to taste

Directions:

To make meatballs:

1. Add beef, parmesan cheese, egg, mozzarella,

garlic, parsley, pepper and salt into a bowl and mix until well combined.
2. Divide the mixture into 8 equal portions and shape into meatballs.
3. Place a skillet over medium flame. Add oil. Swirl the pan so that the oil spreads.
4. Once oil is heated, add meatballs and cook until golden brown all over. Remove the meatballs and set on a plate with layers of paper towels on it.

To make sauce:

1. Place the same pan back over medium heat. Add onion and cook until translucent.
2. Add garlic and oregano and stir continuously for a few seconds until aromatic, taking care not to burn the oregano.
3. Stir in the tomatoes, pepper, and salt and cook for 10 – 12 minutes.
4. Add the meatballs back into the pan. Mix until the meatballs are well coated in the sauce.
5. Reduce the heat to low heat. Cover and cook for about 15 minutes or until the sauce is

thick. Stir every 7 – 8 minutes. Turn off the heat.

<u>To make zucchini noodles:</u>

1. Meanwhile, make noodles of the zucchini using a spiralizer or julienne peeler.
2. Place a pan over medium heat. Add oil. When the oil is heated, add garlic and cook for a few seconds until fragrant.
3. Stir in the zucchini noodles and heat thoroughly. Cook for longer if you like it soft.
4. Serve meatballs and sauce over zucchini noodles. Sprinkle parmesan on top and serve.

Grilled Chicken and Spinach Pizza

Number of servings: 1

Preparation time: 10 minutes

Cooking time: 15 minutes

Ingredients:

<u>For chicken and spinach:</u>

- ½ chicken breast, skinless, boneless
- 2 small cloves garlic, minced
- 1/8 teaspoon xanthan gum
- ¼ cup part-skim mozzarella cheese, shredded
- 1 teaspoon olive oil
- Sea salt to taste
- ¼ cup half and half or heavy whipping cream
- ½ cup chopped fresh spinach
- Pepper to taste

For fathead dough for pizza crust:

- 10 ounces cream cheese
- ½ egg, beaten (beat an egg and use only half of it)
- 3 tablespoons almond flour
- 6 tablespoons shredded mozzarella cheese
- 1/8 teaspoon garlic powder

Directions:

To make pizza crust with fathead dough:

1. Add cream cheese and mozzarella cheese into a microwave safe bowl.
2. Microwave on high in increments of 30

seconds. Stir at the end of 30 seconds. Hopefully it should melt in about a minute. Remove the bowl from the microwave.
3. Add egg, almond flour, and garlic powder into another bowl. Whisk until well combined.
4. Add the melted cheese mixture into it. Mix until well combined. You will have sticky dough.
5. Cover the bowl with plastic wrap and refrigerate for a while.

To make chicken and spinach:

1. Place a skillet over medium flame. Add oil. When the oil is heated, add chicken and sauté until cooked through.
2. Remove chicken and set aside on a plate lined with paper towels.
3. Place the skillet back over medium flame. Add garlic, xanthan gum and half and half, and stir.
4. When it begins to boil, lower the heat and simmer until the mixture thickens.
5. Add spinach and stir. Cook for a couple of

minutes until spinach wilts. Turn off the heat.

6. Remove the dough from the refrigerator.

To bake the pizza:

1. Grease a pizza pan with some cooking spray. Place the dough in the prepared pizza pan. Spread it into a disc depending on how thick you want the crust to be.
2. Set the temperature of the oven to 350° F and preheat.
3. Place the baking sheet in the oven. Set the timer for 10 minutes.
4. Remove the pizza pan from the oven. Spread the spinach mixture over the crust.
5. Place chicken (chop the chicken into smaller pieces if desired) on the crust. Sprinkle cheese on top.
6. Bake for 5-6 minutes until the cheese melts.
7. Slice into wedges and serve.

Hearty Chicken Stew with Fries

Number of servings: 8

Preparation time: 20 minutes

Cooking time: 45 minutes

Ingredients:

For chicken stew:

- 2 pounds chicken breasts, skinless, boneless, rinsed
- 2 medium carrots, sliced into rounds
- ½ green bell pepper, chopped into 1 inch squares
- ½ red bell pepper, chopped into 1 inch squares
- 1 ripe tomato, chopped
- 12 fresh mushrooms, sliced
- 2 stalks celery, chopped
- 2 cloves garlic, minced
- ¼ cup low carb tomato sauce
- 4 tablespoons butter, unsalted
- 2 bay leaves, crumbled
- 2 sticks cinnamon
- 4 teaspoons whole peppercorns
- 2 teaspoons white pepper powder
- 2 tablespoons olive oil
- Salt to taste
- 6 cups water

To make fries:

- 2 large swede, peeled, cut into fries
- 1 teaspoon paprika
- Sea salt to taste
- 4 tablespoons extra-virgin olive oil or any other oil of your choice
- Freshly ground pepper to taste
- ½ teaspoon ground cloves (optional)

Directions:

To make stew:

1. Place chicken pieces in a bowl and season with salt. Set aside.
2. Place a soup pot over medium heat. Add oil and butter. When butter melts, add the whole peppercorns, cinnamon, and bay leaves. Sauté for about 8-10 seconds.
3. Stir in the garlic. Stir for 15 – 20 seconds until the garlic is fragrant.
4. Stir in the onion and cook until onions turn golden brown.
5. Stir in the tomatoes. Cook until the tomatoes are soft. Stir occasionally.

6. Add tomato paste and mix well. Lower the heat to low and cook for about a minute.
7. Add celery, chicken, mushrooms, carrot and salt, and stir.
8. Raise the heat to medium and let the mixture come to a boil.
9. Lower the heat once again and cover the pot. Cook until the chicken is nearly cooked through.
10. Add the red and green bell peppers and simmer uncovered for about 5 minutes. Stir frequently.
11. Ladle into bowls and serve hot with fries.

To make fries:

1. While the stew is cooking, set the temperature of the oven to 465° F and preheat the oven.
2. Dry the fries by patting with paper towels.
3. Add oil, salt, cloves, paprika and salt into a bowl and stir well. Add the swede fries into the bowl and stir until well coated.
4. Line a baking sheet with parchment paper. Spread the fries on the baking sheet.
5. Place the baking sheet in the oven and bake

for 25 – 30 minutes or until crisp. You can also make fries with parsnip, celery root, turnip, kohlrabi, parsley root, etc.
6. Remove the baking sheet from the oven and serve right away.

Keto Chicken Pot Pie

Number of servings: 4

Preparation time: 20 minutes

Cooking time: 22 minutes

Ingredients:

For chicken pot pie filling:

- 1 tablespoon butter
- 2 tablespoons diced onion
- 1/8 teaspoon pepper or to taste
- 6 tablespoons heavy whipping cream
- ½ teaspoon poultry seasoning
- 1/8 teaspoon thyme
- 1/8 teaspoon xanthan gum
- ¼ cup mixed vegetables of your choice
- 1/8 teaspoon Himalayan pink salt
- 1 clove garlic, peeled, minced
- ½ cup chicken broth

- 1/8 teaspoon rosemary
- 1 ¼ cups cooked, diced chicken

For crust:

- 2 ¼ tablespoons butter, melted, cooled
- 1 tablespoon full fat sour cream
- 1/8 teaspoon salt
- ½ cup grated mild cheddar cheese
- Finely chopped parsley, to garnish
- 3 tablespoons coconut flour
- 2 eggs
- 1/8 teaspoon baking powder
- 3 tablespoons grated mozzarella cheese

Directions:

1. Place an ovenproof skillet over medium heat. Add butter. When butter melts, add onion and cook until soft.
2. Stir in chicken broth, heavy whipping cream, thyme, poultry seasoning, and rosemary.
3. Scatter xanthan gum on top. Cover and reduce the heat to low. Cook for 4 to 5 minutes.
4. Stir in the chicken. Cover and let it simmer.

5. Set the temperature of the oven to 400° F and preheat the oven.

To make crust:

1. Add butter, salt, eggs and sour cream into a bowl and whisk well.
2. Stir in baking powder and coconut flour. Next, add cheese and mix well.
3. If you think that there is too little liquid in the skillet, add some more broth because the batter will absorb some of the liquid from the pan.
4. Drop spoonfuls of the batter all over the top of the potpie. Turn off the heat.
5. Place the skillet in the oven. Set the timer for 15 minutes and let it bake.
6. Now set the oven to broil mode. Shift the skillet to the top shelf. Broil for a couple of minutes.
7. Garnish with parsley and serve.

Keto Cheeseburger

Number of servings: 2

Preparation time: 15 minutes

Cooking time: 45 – 50 minutes

Ingredients:

For burger patties:

- 10.4 ounces ground beef
- 1 teaspoon onion powder
- ½ teaspoon sea salt
- ½ tablespoon ghee or lard
- 2 small cloves garlic, peeled, minced
- ½ teaspoon apple cider vinegar
- ½ teaspoon pepper

For burger sauce:

- 2 tablespoons keto friendly mayonnaise
- ½ tablespoon pickle juice or lemon juice
- 1 tablespoon sugar-free ketchup or tomato puree
- Pepper to taste
- Salt to taste

To assemble:

- 2 keto buns
- 2 slices bacon, cut lengthwise

- 8 slices sugar-free pickles
- 2 tomato slices
- 1 tablespoon butter, melted
- 1 cup shredded lettuce
- 4 slices onion
- 2 slices cheddar cheese or Monterey Jack cheese or provolone cheese
- Ghee to grease the pan

For burger buns: Makes 5 buns

- ¾ cup almond flour
- ¼ cup coconut flour
- 1/3 cup psyllium husk (measure first and then grind it into fine powder)
- ¼ cup packed flaxseed meal
- 1 teaspoon onion powder
- ½ teaspoon baking soda
- 2 ½ tablespoons sesame seeds or poppy seeds or flax seeds or sunflower seeds
- 1 teaspoon garlic powder
- 1 teaspoon cream of tartar or apple cider vinegar
- ½ teaspoon Himalayan pink salt
- ½ - 1 tablespoon erythritol or swerve
- 1 large egg

- 3 egg whites
- 1 cup boiling water

Directions:

To make keto buns:

1. Add almond flour, coconut flour, flax meal, garlic powder, psyllium husk powder, onion powder, baking soda, cream of tartar, erythritol, and salt into a mixing bowl and stir until well combined.
2. Mix in the egg and egg whites using an electric hand mixer. The dough will be thick.
3. Place a sheet of parchment paper on a baking sheet.
4. Pour boiling water and mix until well incorporated. Divide the dough into 5 equal portions. Shape into buns and place on the prepared baking sheet. Leave sufficient gap between the buns.
5. Sprinkle sesame seeds on top. Press the seeds to adhere.
6. Set the temperature of the oven to 400° F and preheat the oven.
7. Place the baking sheet in the oven and set the timer for about 35 – 40 minutes and

bake the buns. Keep a watch on the buns after about 25 minutes of baking so they do not burn.
8. Take out the baking sheet from the oven and let it cool. Use as many as required and store the rest in an airtight container. It can last for 2 days at room temperature. You can place it in the refrigerator as well. It will last for 4 – 5 days.

<u>To make burger patties:</u>

1. Add beef, onion powder, apple cider vinegar, pepper, garlic and salt into a bowl and stir until just combined. Do not mix for long, or else you will end up with tough burgers.
2. Divide the mixture into 2 equal portions and shape into patties. Prick with a fork, all over the patties. Place on a plate lined with parchment paper.

<u>To make sauce:</u>

1. Add mayonnaise, pickle juice, pepper, ketchup and salt into a bowl and stir well.

2. Place a skillet over medium heat. Let it heat up.
3. Split the keto buns horizontally and place in the skillet, with the cut side touching the bottom of the skillet. Cook until crisp. Remove the buns and set aside.
4. Add ghee into the skillet and let it melt. Raise the heat to high. Place the burger patties on the pan and cook until it becomes brown at the bottom. Flip sides and cook the other side until brown.
5. Remove burgers and set aside on a plate.
6. Add bacon into the same skillet and cook until crisp.

To assemble:

1. Spread burger sauce on the cut side of the buns. Place 4 slices of pickles on each of the bottom halves of the buns. Divide the lettuce among the buns.
2. Place the burgers over the lettuce followed by cheese, tomato slices, and onion slices. Cover with the top half of the buns.
3. Serve.

Keto Low Carb Lasagna with Garlic Broccoli

Number of servings: 2

Preparation time: 15 minutes

Cooking time: 45 – 50 minutes

Ingredients:

For cheese dough lasagna noodles:

- 2 ounces full fat cream cheese, at room temperature
- 1 large egg
- ¾ cup shredded, part-skim low moisture mozzarella cheese
- ½ teaspoon Italian seasoning

For lasagna filling:

- 2 tablespoons minced onion
- ½ cup keto friendly marinara sauce
- 3 tablespoons ricotta cheese
- ½ pound ground beef
- ½ teaspoon Italian seasoning
- ½ cup shredded, low moisture, part-skim mozzarella cheese

For garlic broccoli:

- ½ pound broccoli florets
- 4 teaspoons fresh lemon juice
- Salt to taste
- 1 ½ tablespoons olive oil
- ¼ teaspoon garlic powder

To serve:

- Freshly grated parmesan cheese
- Finely chopped fresh herbs like oregano, basil, parsley etc.

Directions:

To make cheese dough lasagna noodles:

1. Place a sheet of parchment paper in a baking dish (size 8 x 8 inches).
2. Add cream cheese, egg, mozzarella cheese and Italian seasoning into the food processor bowl. Process until well combined. You will have a thick batter. You can also mix with your hands.
3. Spoon the batter into the prepared baking dish. Spread it evenly with a spatula.

4. Place a rack in the center of the oven.
5. Set the temperature of the oven to 350° F and preheat the oven.
6. Place the baking dish in the oven and set the timer for about 20 minutes or until set.
7. Remove the baking dish from the oven and let it cool. Cut into 3 equal slices.

To make meat sauce filling:

1. Place a skillet over medium heat. Add onion and meat and cook until beef is brown. Break it simultaneously as it cooks.
2. Discard extra cooked fat from the pan.
3. Stir in marinara sauce and Italian sauce. Lower the heat to low. Simmer for a couple of minutes.

To assemble:

1. Take another baking pan, the size of the lasagna noodle slices. A loaf pan would work well.
2. Spread a thin layer of the meat sauce on the bottom of the baking pan. Place a slice of lasagna noodle over it.

3. Spread 1/3 of the meat sauce over the lasagna noodle. Scatter 1 ½ tablespoons ricotta cheese followed by 2 tablespoons mozzarella cheese.
4. Place another noodle. Follow steps 2 and 3 again.
5. Place the 3rd noodle. Spread remaining meat sauce followed by remaining mozzarella cheese. Sprinkle Italian seasoning and any other seasonings if desired in the layers.
6. Place the baking dish in the oven. Set the timer for 20 minutes. If you want the top to be brown, broil for a couple of minutes.
7. Remove the baking dish from the oven. Let it cool for 5 minutes.
8. Garnish with parmesan cheese and fresh herbs.
9. Cut into 2 equal slices and serve.

To make garlic broccoli:

1. While the lasagna is baking, place a skillet over medium heat.
2. Add oil and let it heat. Add broccoli and cook for a few minutes until it turns bright

green. Add garlic powder and salt and mix well. Turn off the heat.
3. Add lemon juice and toss well.

Beef Tacos

Number of servings: 2

Preparation time: 20 minutes

Cooking time: 20 minutes

Ingredients:

For taco shells:

- ¼ teaspoon ground cumin
- 1 cup shredded cheddar cheese

For filling:

- Taco seasoning to taste
- ¼ teaspoon salt
- ½ avocado, peeled, pitted, diced
- ¼ cup shredded cheddar cheese
- ½ pound ground beef
- ½ cup shredded lettuce
- Pepper to taste
- ¼ cup diced tomatoes

Directions:

To make taco shells:

1. Place a sheet of parchment paper on a baking sheet. Divide the cheese into 2 equal portions. Scatter each portion to form a circle of about 6 inches.
2. Set the temperature of the oven to 350° F and preheat the oven.
3. Place the baking sheet in the oven and set the timer for about 6 – 8 minutes, until light brown. Keep a watch on the buns after about 5 minutes of baking so that they do not burn.
4. Remove the baking sheet from the oven and let it cool for about 2 minutes.
5. Balance a wooden spoon with a long handle between 2 cups placed on either side of the spoon.
6. Lift the melted cheese circles and place them on the handle of the spoon. Lightly bend the cheese rounds if necessary to give the shape of a taco shell.
7. Let them cool completely on the handle. Once they cool completely, your taco shells will be ready.

<u>To make taco filling:</u>

1. Place a skillet over medium-high flame. Add beef and cook until brown. Break it as it cooks. Add salt, pepper, and taco seasoning to taste.
2. Divide equally the taco filling and place in the taco shells. Scatter some lettuce, tomatoes, avocado and cheese over the filling and serve.

Cheeseburger Helper with Kale Brussels sprouts Salad

Number of servings: 2

Preparation time: 10 minutes

Cooking time: 35 minutes

Ingredients:

<u>For beef and cabbage:</u>

- ½ pound ground beef (80/20)
- ¼ teaspoon onion powder
- ½ teaspoon paprika
- 1/8 teaspoon garlic powder
- ½ tablespoon tomato paste

- Pepper to taste
- 1 cup shredded cabbage
- 2 tablespoons water
- Salt to taste

For cheese sauce:

- 1 tablespoon salted butter
- ¼ cup heavy whipping cream
- Pepper to taste
- Salt to taste
- ½ ounce cream cheese, at room temperature
- ¾ cup shredded cheddar cheese
- Cooked, crumbled bacon, to garnish (optional)

For kale Brussels sprouts salad:

- 3 – 4 cups curly kale leaves
- ¼ cup sugar-free, dried cranberries
- ¼ cup walnuts or pumpkin seeds
- 1 ½ cups Brussels sprouts, discard outer leaves and stems
- 3 slices cooked bacon, chopped
- 2 tablespoons blue cheese crumbles
- 3 tablespoons olive oil

- ½ tablespoon Dijon mustard
- Sea salt to taste
- 1 tablespoon lemon juice
- ¼ teaspoon garlic powder
- 1/8 teaspoon pepper powder

Directions:

To make beef:

1. Place a skillet over medium heat. Add beef and cook until it is not pink anymore.
2. Discard extra fat from the pan.
3. Add onion powder, paprika, garlic powder, tomato paste, pepper, cabbage, water and salt and mix well. Cover and cook until cabbage is cooked. Stir occasionally.

To make cheese sauce:

1. While the meat and cabbage are cooking, add butter into a saucepan.
2. Place the saucepan over medium heat. Once the butter melts, add heavy whipping cream and cream cheese and whisk well.
3. Lower the heat to low. Add cheese, salt, and

pepper and stir. Remove from heat. Stir constantly until the cheese melts completely.
4. Add the cheese sauce into the pan of beef and mix well.
5. Garnish with bacon and serve with kale Brussels sprouts salad.

To make Brussels sprouts salad:

1. Fit the food processor with a fine slicer blade. With the machine running, add the Brussels sprouts into the feeder tube. Press with the pusher.
2. Next add the kale into the feeder tube. Press with the pusher.
3. Transfer into a bowl. Also add cranberries, walnuts, bacon and blue cheese crumbles and toss well.

To make dressing:

1. Add olive oil, Dijon mustard, salt, lemon juice, garlic powder, and pepper into a bowl and whisk well. The dressing should get emulsified.

2. Pour the dressing over the salad and fold gently.

Chicken and Waffles

Number of servings: 2

Preparation time: 20 minutes

Cooking time: 45 minutes

Ingredients:

For fried chicken tenderloins:

- Coconut oil or avocado oil, to fry
- ½ pound chicken tenderloins

For chicken marinade:

- ½ cup heavy whipping cream
- ½ tablespoon apple cider vinegar
- ½ teaspoon salt or to taste
- 4 teaspoons Tabasco hot sauce
- Pepper to taste

For breading chicken:

- ¼ cup fine almond flour, sifted
- 2 tablespoons finely grated parmesan cheese
- 2 tablespoons coconut flour
- ½ teaspoon paprika
- ¼ teaspoon cayenne pepper or to taste
- ¼ teaspoon onion powder
- ¼ teaspoon garlic powder
- ½ teaspoon salt
- Pepper to taste
- 1 large egg, beaten, for egg wash

For Belgium waffles:

- 4 ounces full- fat cream cheese
- 4 – 6 tablespoons water
- 2 tablespoons coconut flour

- 1 tablespoon granulated swerve
- 1 teaspoon baking powder
- ¼ teaspoon salt
- 3 small eggs, at room temperature
- ½ cup super-fine almond flour
- ½ tablespoon psyllium husk powder
- 1/8 teaspoon pepper

For cayenne maple syrup:

- 6 tablespoons sugar-free maple syrup (recipe is given in Breakfast chapter – Crispy cinnamon waffles)
- 2 tablespoons cold, unsalted butter
- ½ teaspoon Tabasco sauce

Directions:

To prepare the chicken:

1. Place a sheet of plastic wrap on your countertop. Place chicken over it. Place another sheet of plastic wrap over the chicken.
2. Pound the chicken lightly with a meat mallet until flat. Rinse the chicken well and dry by patting with paper towels.

To make marinade:

1. Add heavy cream, vinegar, salt, hot sauce, and pepper into a bowl. Whisk until well combined.
2. Place chicken in the marinade and turn the chicken around to coat it well with the marinade. Place the bowl covered, in the refrigerator, for 2 – 8 hours.

For breading:

1. Make the breading mixture after you remove the bowl from the refrigerator, to make the chicken.
2. Add almond flour, parmesan cheese, coconut flour, paprika, cayenne pepper, onion powder, garlic powder, salt, and pepper into a bowl and stir.
3. First dip the chicken pieces in egg, one at a time. Shaking off excess egg, dredge in the flour mixture. Shake to drop off excess flour and place on a plate.
4. Place a pan over medium-high heat. Add 4 – 5 tablespoons coconut oil or avocado oil. When the oil is heated, place chicken in the

pan and cook until the underside is light brown. Flip sides and cook the other side until light brown. Cook in batches if required, adding more oil in the next batch if required.

5. Remove and place on a baking sheet. Cover the baking sheet loosely with foil.
6. Set the temperature of the oven to 350° F and preheat the oven.
7. Place the baking sheet in the oven and set the timer for about 20 minutes, until the chicken is cooked well inside.

<u>To make Belgian waffles:</u>

1. Plug in the waffle maker and preheat it following the manufacturer's instructions.
2. Add all the dry ingredients (almond flour, baking powder, psyllium husk powder, coconut flour and sweetener) into a bowl and stir until well combined.
3. Add cream cheese into a mixing bowl and whisk lightly using an electric hand mixer.
4. Add the eggs, one at a time, and whisk well each time. Scrape the sides of the bowl whenever required.

5. Add the mixture of dry ingredients into the bowl of eggs. Stir until well combined using a spatula.
6. Add water and stir until well combined.
7. Pour half the batter into the preheated waffle maker. Set the timer for about 7 – 8 minutes. Close the waffle maker.
8. Check after about 5 minutes. Cook until crisp and golden brown. Take out the waffle when cooked and set aside on a plate. Let it sit for a couple of minutes.
9. Cook the other waffle similarly.

To make cayenne maple syrup:

1. Add sugar-free maple syrup into a small saucepan. Place the saucepan over medium low heat. When it begins to bubble, add Tabasco sauce and stir. Remove from heat.
2. Add butter and stir.
3. Place waffles on individual serving plates. Place chicken over the waffles. Drizzle cayenne maple syrup on top and serve.

Beef Stew with Herby Dumplings Served with Mashed Cauliflower Celery Root

Number of servings: 3 (with 2 dumplings each)

Preparation time: 10 minutes

Cooking time: 2 – 3 hours

Ingredients:

For stew:

- 1 pound stewing beef meat
- ½ medium red onion, chopped
- ½ medium carrot, cut into cubes
- 2 sprigs fresh rosemary
- 1 tablespoon tomato puree
- 1 cup beef stock or beef bone broth
- Freshly cracked pepper to taste
- 1 tablespoon extra-virgin olive oil or ghee
- 3.5 ounces pumpkin, chopped into cubes
- 2 small bay leaves
- 1 clove garlic, peeled, minced
- ¼ cup dry red wine
- Sea salt or Himalayan pink salt to taste

For dumplings:

- 1 small egg
- 2 small egg whites

- ½ cup boiling water
- 3 tablespoons sesame flour
- 1 ¼ tablespoons psyllium husk powder
- 2 tablespoons almond flour
- 2 tablespoons coconut flour
- 1/8 teaspoon Himalayan pink salt
- ¾ teaspoon baking powder
- ½ tablespoon chopped fresh thyme
- ½ tablespoon chopped fresh rosemary

For mashed cauliflower with celery root:

- 7 ounces celeriac, peeled, cubed
- ¾ pound cauliflower florets
- 2 small cloves garlic, peeled, sliced
- 3 ounces butter
- ½ tablespoon chopped chives or green onion or parsley (optional)
- 4 tablespoons heavy cream or sour cream or buttermilk
- Pepper to taste
- Cooked bacon or cheddar cheese to garnish

To serve:

- ½ teaspoon grated, fresh lemon zest

- A handful fresh parsley, chopped, to garnish
- Cracked pepper
- Mashed cauliflower with celery root

Directions:

To make stew:

1. Place a pan over medium heat. Add ½ tablespoon oil and let it heat.
2. Add stewing beef meat and cook until brown. Stir frequently. Remove the meat from the pan and set aside in a bowl. Wipe the pan.
3. Set the temperature of the oven to 330° F. Place a casserole dish in the oven and preheat the oven.
4. Place the pan back over heat. Add remaining oil. When the oil is heated, add onion, carrot and pumpkin and cook until slightly tender.
5. Stir in the beef, garlic, rosemary, thyme, tomato puree, and bay leaves. Stir-fry for a couple of minutes.
6. Stir in the red wine. Lower the heat and cook for 3 – 4 minutes.
7. Stir in the stock, salt, and pepper. Once it begins to boil, turn off the heat. Transfer the

stew into a casserole dish. Close the lid of the casserole dish.

8. Place the casserole dish in the oven and set the timer for about 2 hours. Cook until the meat is cooked through. It can take longer to cook. Once done, remove the casserole dish from the oven.

<u>To make dumplings:</u>

1. In the meantime, whisk together whole and egg whites in a bowl, with a fork.
2. Add all the dry ingredients (coconut flour, almond flour, salt, baking powder, psyllium husk powder and sesame flour) into a bowl and stir until well combined.
3. Add eggs and mix with an electric hand mixer until well incorporated.
4. Pour boiling water and mix until well incorporated.
5. Increase the temperature of the oven to 350° F. Grease a 6 count muffin pan with some oil.
6. Divide the dough into 6 equal portions and shape into dumplings. Place the dumplings in the prepared muffin cups.

7. Set the timer for 25 minutes and bake the dumplings. Flip the dumplings and bake for another 5 minutes.

To make mashed cauliflower and celery root:

1. While the dumplings are baking, add celeriac and garlic into a pot. Pour enough water to cover the celeriac. Place the pot over high heat and cook until tender. Turn off the heat and discard the water.
2. Add cauliflower into a microwave safe bowl. Sprinkle a little water over the cauliflower. Place the bowl in the microwave. Microwave on high for 5 minutes or until tender. Discard the water.
3. Add heavy cream, cauliflower, garlic, and celeriac into the food processor bowl. Process until smooth. Add salt, pepper, and butter, and pulse until well combined.
4. Add chives and stir. Transfer into a serving bowl.
5. Reheat the stew if necessary. Drop the baked dumplings in the stew. Mix well.

To serve:

1. Ladle the stew in bowls.
2. Garnish with lemon zest, pepper, and parsley and serve with mashed cauliflower celery root.

Keto Steak with Béarnaise Sauce and Herbed Smashed Cucumbers

Number of servings: 2

Preparation time: 15 minutes

Cooking time: 15 minutes

Ingredients:

For béarnaise sauce:

- 1 teaspoon white wine vinegar
- 1 tablespoon finely chopped fresh tarragon
- Pepper to taste
- 5 ounces butter
- Salt to taste
- 2 egg yolks, at room temperature
- ¼ teaspoon onion powder

For steak:

- 2 rib eye steaks (about 1 pound), at room temperature
- Salt to taste
- 1 tablespoon butter
- Pepper to taste

For herb smashed cucumbers:

- 2 tablespoons whole milk plain Greek yogurt
- ½ tablespoon olive oil
- ¼ cup finely chopped red onions
- ½ tablespoon chopped fresh parsley leaves
- Freshly ground pepper to taste
- ½ tablespoon fresh lemon juice
- 1 pound cucumbers, peeled, halved lengthwise, cut into 1 inch pieces crosswise
- ½ tablespoon coarsely chopped dill fronds
- Flaky salt to taste

Directions:

To make béarnaise sauce:

1. Add onion powder, vinegar, and tarragon into a small bowl and whisk well.

2. Add yolks into a heatproof bowl. Beat with an electric hand mixer on low speed.
3. Add butter into a microwave safe bowl and microwave on high for 20 – 30 seconds or until it just melts.
4. Whisking the yolks constantly, pour melted butter into the yolks. Raise the speed once the sauce starts getting thicker.
5. Add vinegar, onion powder, salt, pepper, and tarragon and whisk well. The sauce should be kept warm. For this you can place it on low simmer in a double boiler.

To cook steak:

1. Place a pan over medium heat. Add butter and let it melt.
2. Place steak in the pan. Season with salt and pepper and cook to the desired doneness, i.e. rare cooked, medium cooked, or well cooked.
3. You can also grill it in a preheated grill if desired.
4. Drizzle béarnaise sauce on top and serve with herb smashed cucumbers.

To make herb smashed cucumbers:

1. Add yogurt, oil and lemon juice into a bowl and whisk well.
2. Place the cucumber pieces on your cutting board, cut side facing down. With a pestle, smash the cucumber pieces.
3. Place the smashed cucumbers in a bowl. Also add dill, red onion, parsley, pepper and flaky sea salt and toss well.
4. Drizzle yogurt mixture over it. Toss well. Taste and add more salt and pepper if required.

Keto Nachos

Number of servings: 2

Preparation time: 15 minutes

Cooking time: 15 minutes

Ingredients:

For ground beef:

- 4.4 ounces ground beef
- 2 small cloves garlic, finely minced
- 1 slice bacon, chopped (optional)

- ¼ teaspoon dried oregano
- 1/8 teaspoon garlic powder
- Freshly ground pepper to taste
- Extra-virgin olive oil or avocado oil, to cook
- 1 small onion, very finely chopped
- ½ teaspoon paprika
- ¼ teaspoon ground cumin
- Kosher salt to taste

<u>For tortilla chips:</u> Makes 8 - 10 servings

- 1.7 ounces coconut flour
- 6.8 ounces almond flour
- 2 teaspoons baking powder
- 4 teaspoons xanthan gum
- 4 teaspoons apple cider vinegar
- 6 teaspoons water
- 2 eggs, lightly beaten
- ½ teaspoon kosher salt or to taste
- Oil, to fry, as required

<u>For Dorito dust:</u> Optional

- 2 tablespoons nutritional yeast
- 1 teaspoon dried oregano
- ½ teaspoon onion powder

- Kosher salt to taste
- ¼ teaspoon ground cumin
- ½ tablespoon paprika
- 1 teaspoon garlic powder
- 1 teaspoon chipotle chili powder
- Freshly ground pepper to taste

For serving: Use any

- 4.4 ounces pepper Jack cheese or cheddar cheese
- Few black olives, sliced
- Sliced jalapeños
- Mexican crema or sour cream
- Pico de Gallo
- Guacamole
- Salsa

Directions:

To make tortilla dough:

1. Add coconut flour, almond flour, baking powder, xanthan gum and salt into the food processor bowl. Process until well incorporated.
2. With the machine running, add apple cider

vinegar. When it gets well mixed, add eggs. When eggs are well mixed, add water and process until dough is formed.

3. Cut a large sheet of plastic wrap and wrap the dough in it. Knead the dough along with the plastic wrap for a couple of minutes.
4. Let the dough sit for 10 minutes.
5. Divide the dough into 16 equal portions and shape into balls.
6. Place a sheet of parchment paper on your countertop. Place a ball of dough over it. Cover with another sheet of parchment paper. Roll with a rolling pin or with a tortilla press until thin. If you roll it thick, the tortilla chips will puff up while frying.
7. Cut into 8 triangles.
8. Repeat steps 6 – 7 and make the remaining tortillas.
9. You can either deep fry the tortillas or bake them in an oven, the choice is yours.
10. Place a skillet over medium heat. Add oil and heat.
11. When the oil is well heated and not smoking, and the temperature of the oil reaches 350°F, add a few tortilla chips at a time in the pan and cook until golden brown.

12. Remove and place on a plate lined with paper towels. In case the tortilla chips puff up, remove the puffed ones out from the pan when they are still white in color and place on a baking sheet.
13. Bake in a preheated oven at 400° F for about 8 to 10 minutes until golden brown.

To make Dorito dust (if using):

1. Add nutritional yeast, oregano, onion powder, salt, cumin, paprika, garlic powder, chipotle chili powder and pepper into the blender jar. Blend until smooth. Dust with Dorito dust if desired.
2. If you want to bake the tortilla chips, spread the chips in a single layer on a couple of baking sheets.
3. Bake in a preheated oven at 400°F for about 12 to 15 minutes until golden brown. Flip sides half way through baking.
4. Transfer into an airtight container until use. Use as many as required for making nachos. The rest can be served as snacks or used in some other recipe.

To make beef:

1. Place a skillet over medium heat. Add oil. When the oil is heated, add garlic, bacon and onion and cook until onion turns light brown.
2. Stir in the beef. Add oregano, garlic powder, pepper, paprika and salt and mix well. When beef is cooked well, remove from heat. Drain off extra fat and cooked juices from the pan.

To assemble:

1. Set the oven to broil mode.
2. Place a layer of tortilla chips (6 – 8 chips) in an ovenproof skillet. Scatter beef, olives, and cheese. Repeat the layer once again.
3. Broil for a couple of minutes until the cheese melts.
4. Serve right away with any of the suggested toppings, or else the tortilla chips will get soggy.

CONCLUSION

Being a parent is a full-time responsibility, and there are no breaks or vacations. There are several things you are responsible for, such as your child's physical health, mental well-being, academic performance, and pretty much anything else that you can think of. One important aspect of their life that you need to pay a lot of attention to is their nutrition. Childhood is an incredibly important phase of their life and the nutrition they derive during this period essentially dictates their physical and mental health.

Several parents find it difficult to get their children to eat healthier foods instead of the junk food they all love. Junk food is not just convenient, but it is easily attainable and addictive, too. Apart from this, it's filled with unhealthy fats, carbs, and sugars that

CONCLUSION

enhance the overall taste. Junk food is devoid of all the nourishment and is filled with chemicals and artificial additives that have absolutely no nutritional value whatsoever. However, as a parent, understand the simple fact that the key to changing your child's eating habits lies in your hands. It is not just your responsibility, but also your duty as a parent to make sure that your child's diet is filled with nutrient-dense foods instead of empty calories. To regain control of the situation and improve your child's health, it is time you follow the protocols of the keto diet.

The keto diet is quite simple to follow and the only rule you must keep in mind is to increase your child's intake of healthy fats and reduce carbs and sugars from their diet. As long as you follow this protocol, there is nothing else that you need to do. This high-fat and low carb eating pattern will improve your child's overall health. From reducing the chances and risk of harmful chronic illnesses to improving their heart health, and stabilizing their overall energy levels, this diet is the key to better health.

Also, the keto diet helps tackle childhood obesity along with assisting in weight loss and weight management. Any of the possible side effects of this diet can be easily managed. To manage and even avoid the symptoms of the keto flu, encourage your child to drink plenty of water. Ensure that they get sufficient sleep and rest, and keep an eye on their intake of electrolytes. It takes anywhere between a week and ten days to get used to this diet. Once your child's body is acclimatized to this diet, you don't have to worry about their overall nutrition.

Nutrition is extremely important for all stages of life and even more so for a growing child. The nourishment your child receives in their childhood essentially dictates their overall health. It also determines the relationship they have with food. If you don't want to raise a fussy eater, then encourage your child to experiment with food and try everything. To get your child used to this diet, follow a schedule, ensure that your child eats breakfast, lunch, and dinner, get creative with recipes, use alternatives to junk food, allow them to eat occasional treats, and model good behavior.

In this book, you were also given a detailed food list, so follow it whenever you shop for groceries. Ensure that at least 70 to 75% of your child's daily calorie intake comes from dietary fats, about 20% from

CONCLUSION

proteins, and the rest from carbs. The ketogenic diet is not restrictive, and it offers plenty of variety. As long as you get creative and don't limit yourself in the kitchen, your child will get to eat a variety of foods. To make things easier, follow the simple meal prep. So, plan all the meals for a week, set some time aside for meal prep, check for overlapping ingredients, cook food properly, and store it for later.

Once everything is in place, it is time to slowly get your child used to this diet. As with anything else in life, change becomes easier when it is not drastic. When you gradually introduce your child to this diet, the likelihood of them liking it increases. Slowly eliminate some types of carbs from their daily meals, get them involved in cooking, stay organized, and deal with their picky eating habits. It is not difficult to follow this diet.

Everything that you need about this diet is provided within this book. From understanding what the ketogenic diet needs to how it works and myths about it along with the various benefits it offers, this book includes everything. You were also given some simple yet practical tips you can use to easily transition your child to the keto diet. Apart from all this, this book also included several keto-friendly recipes.

CONCLUSION

From quick and easy breakfast to delicious and scrumptious lunches and dinners, there is plenty of variety to choose from. All these recipes are incredibly simple to understand and easy to cook. You don't have to slave away in the kitchen to cook healthy, delicious, and nutritious meals for your kid. With a little meal prep, cooking will become a breeze.

Now, all that's left for you to do is gather the necessary supplies and the ingredients, make a meal plan for your child, and get started. All the 40 recipes given in this book are easy to make and incredibly delicious. Also, they are perfect for not just the meals your child has a home, but can also be packed for school lunch. When you introduce your child to this diet, be prepared for a little resistance initially. However, don't give up and be a little patient. Your resilience, patience, and effort will not go to waste, especially when you see an improvement in your child's overall health. It is never too late to take action, and there is no time like the present to get started. Eating healthier meals doesn't have to be a chore on the keto diet.

REFERENCES

A. A. Gibson, R. V. Seimon, C. M. Y. Lee, J. Ayre, J. Franklin, T. P. Markovic, I. D. Caterson, A. Sainsbury Obes Rev. 2015 Jan; 16(1): 64–76. Published online 2014 Nov 17. doi: 10.1111/obr.12230

Burns, J. (2019). 15 Ways to Get Your Kids to Eat Better. Retrieved from https://www.parents.com/kids/nutrition/healthy-eating/get-your-kids-to-eat-better/

Jenkinson, L. (2017). HuffPost is now a part of Verizon Media. Retrieved from https://www.huffpost.com/entry/10-myths-about-kids-going-low-carb_b_596352bfe4b0cf3c8e8d5a13

Krikorian, R., Shidler, M. D., Dangelo, K., Couch, S. C., Benoit, S. C., & Clegg, D. J. (2012). Dietary ketosis enhances memory in mild cognitive impairment. *Neurobiology of aging, 33*(2), 425.e19–425.e4.25E27. https://doi.org/10.1016/j.neurobiolaging.2010.10.006

List of Foods to Avoid on Keto | Atkins. Retrieved from https://www.atkins.com/how-it-works/library/articles/helpful-tips-ketogenic-foods-to-avoid

Maria Zick, S., Snyder, D., & Abrams, D. (2018). Pros and Cons of Dietary Strategies Popular Among Cancer Patients. Retrieved from https://www.cancernetwork.com/dietary-strategies-cancer

Walsh, K. (2020). Everything You Can and Can't Eat on the Keto Diet. Retrieved from https://www.womansday.com/health-fitness/nutrition/a25602934/keto-diet-foods/

www.ingramcontent.com/pod-product-compliance
Lightning Source LLC
Chambersburg PA
CBHW071234070526
44583CB00017B/2177